LOOKING THROUGH THE EYES OF A DISCIPLE-MAKER

VOLUME ONE

Herb Hodges

LOOKING THROUGH THE EYES OF A DISCIPLE-MAKER

VOLUME ONE

©2010 Herb Hodges

ALL RIGHTS RESERVED

No part of this publication may be reproduced, stored in a retrieval system, or transmitted in any form without prior written permission.

Spiritual Life Ministries

2916 Old Elm Lane

Germantown, TN 38138

Herb Hodges -- Executive Director

E-mail – herbslm@mindspring.com

Table of Contents

Chapter 1
Living in Four Worlds - 5

Chapter 2
Looking into the Heart of a Disciple-Maker - 21

Chapter 3
Listening to the Prayer of a Disciple-Maker - 45

Chapter 4
God's Surprise Party for the Disciple-Maker - 57

Chapter 5
A Prisoner's Passion - 71

Chapter 6
Christianity Condensed - 81

Chapter 7
Earmarks of a Disciple-Maker - 97

Chapter 8
A Disciple-Maker's Desire for Unity - 111

Chapter 9
From Throne to Throne by Way of the Earth - 127

Chapter 10
Does Obedience Produce Slavery or Freedom? - 149

Chapter 11
Timothy: a Role Model for Disciples &Disciple-Makers - 169

Chapter 12
How Heaven Decorates Its War Heroes - 189

INTRODUCTION

The introductory phrase of the book of Philippians "Paul and Timothy," shows the importance of one disciple-maker, a "trigger" man, a "catalytic" man, an "introducer." Paul could have been an invincible loner. If ever a single individual overthrew an entire society, it was the Apostle Paul. He practically conquered the entire Roman Empire alone. And yet, not alone. Not alone at all. He had the Near Presence of the One who said, "I myself am with you all the days, even to the end of the age." And he always seemed to have around him a cluster of individuals who were pursuing with him "the prize of the high calling of God in Christ Jesus." Paul stood in a long line of world-impacters for many reasons, and one of the most important of them was his understanding and practice of the discipler-disciple relationship and the disciple-making process.

As we look through the eyes of the second greatest disciple-maker in history, (Jesus being the greatest!) we see that two words dominate the book of Philippians. One is the word "Gospel", the other is the word "joy." Gospel is the subject, and joy is the sequel. Gospel is the proclamation, and joy is the product. When a believer in Christ refuses to be monopolized by extraneous (trivial by comparison) things, and *preaches the Gospel to himself* and *practices what he preaches*, he will know the joy of Christ.

Though the word "Gospel" occurs nine times in the brief letter to the Philippians, there is no definition of the word in this letter. Here, the impact of the Gospel in the world and in the lives of believers may be clearly seen. Four of the major "plots" of the "Gospel" may be vividly seen here—the Person of Christ, His Work of Redemption for sinners, His super-exaltation above all things, and how all of this is worked out in human experience.

Chapter 1

Living in Four Worlds

Paul and Timothy, the servants of Jesus Christ, To all the saints in Christ Jesus which are at Philippi, with the bishops and deacons. (Philippians 1:1)

The study of words has always deeply fascinated me. For example, look closely at our English word "environment". We get this word from the Latin language through the French language, and it literally means, "that which surrounds". Any encompassing element of our experience is part of our environment.

Suppose that you are a passenger on the Queen Mary crossing the Atlantic. Around you is *the ship itself,* which is transporting you to your destination. Around you also are *your fellow passengers,* the total list of fellow travelers. They may be kindly, companionable, and helpful--or they may be the opposite of that! But whatever their disposition, when the ship is launched, you are locked in with them for better or worse! Around you, too, is a third environment, and it is very threatening. *The ocean,* at its very best, by its very nature, requires a lot of power to pass through, and at its worst becomes a tremendous threat to the traveler, opposing his safe arrival at the desired harbor. Then there is a fourth environment, which is actually a small and specialized part of environment number two. This fourth environment is comprised of *the individual traveler's circle of intimate associates or companions.* So each traveler has four concentric circles around him as he travels. The largest circle is the ocean, the next is the ship, the third is the total passenger list, and the fourth is the much smaller circle (it could be as few as one) of his intimate companions.

Now take this simple illustration and superimpose it over the text at the beginning of this study. The phrase, "in Christ Jesus", identifies one environment for the Christian. The phrase, "all the saints", identifies a second environment. The phrase, "at Philippi", points our a third environment. And the phrase, "Paul and Timothy", suggests a very important fourth environment.

MY PRIMARY ENVIRONMENT — "In Christ Jesus."

The place of the believer's *primary environment* is specified by the words, "in Christ Jesus." The Christian's life is lived "in Christ Jesus." This phrase is used in Paul's letters no less that 164 times. "If any man be in Christ, he is a new creation." "There is now no condemnation to those who are in Christ Jesus." As a child of God, I am surrounded by Christ, separated unto Christ, sheltered in Christ, and supplied by Christ.

You can ask a man if he is "in business," and he will know what you are talking about. You can ask him if he is in one of the professions, say, law or medicine, and he will know what you are talking about. You can ask him if he is "in love," and he knows quite well what you mean. But many people are strangely mystified by the phrase, "in Christ." And some of them are active church members in evangelical churches! Yet, the early Christians were perfectly at home with this phrase, "in Christ Jesus", and the Christian who would be victorious must be increasingly at home with this phrase, too — and even more at home in the environment defined by this phrase.

Dora Greenwell wrote of a woman of eighty years who passed by faith into this new environment in which one actually experiences the pardon, peace, purpose and power of Jesus Christ. At eighty-four, she wrote these words:

> *"If you ask me how long I have lived in the world,*
> *I'm old, I'm very old.*

If you ask me how long I've truly lived,
It will very soon be told;
Past eighty years of age, Yet only four years old!"

Eighty years in her earthly community, but only four years "in Christ." And the dear lady announced that she had only lived for those four years! No person will be truly alive in any of the other three environments until he is firmly planted by the grace of God in Christ. To be in Christ means that Christ is to the Christian what the ark was to Noah. The flood of Noah's day represents the judgment of God. The waters of that judgment were sealed out, and Noah was sealed inside the ark. The entire world was condemned, but not Noah. He was safe and secure in the ark. The same is true of a believer because he is in Christ. By the grace of God and through faith in Jesus Christ, I have been born "from above". In the moment of my New Birth, I was translated out of Adam and into Christ. I am now "in Christ." This phrase Declares my Position, Determines my Possessions, Dictates my Practice, and Defines my Prospect. There is a vast difference between being in Christ and not being there!

A well-worn illustration will help us see this even more clearly. Two boys grew up together. They were close friends as children, but as they entered their teen years their paths began to diverge and they ended up in very different places. Ernie was always in trouble. He began by shoplifting minor amounts of merchandise from stores, and worked his way up to stealing cars. Next it was armed robbery. Finally, in a robbery attempt, he killed a man. He was arrested, convicted, and sentenced to death. Mike's life, however, took quite a different track. He continued in school, working his way through college. After he graduated, he became a successful businessman. However, he had a lot of difficulty with his physical health. His eyes in particular were very weak. As he grew older, his sight deteriorated until he was legally blind.

One day, Mike heard the news about his old friend Ernie. He had great sorrow and tremendous compassion over what had happened to his old friend, and he reached out to him. He went to visit Ernie in prison. They had a very emotional reunion there, and the old friendship was renewed. And an idea began to form in Ernie's mind. He was about to die, and his friend was sightless. Was it possible that he could do something worthwhile in his death? Could he give his eyes so that his old friend could see? It turned out to be medically possible, and that is what happened. Ernie was executed for his crime, but through surgery his good eyes were used to restore Mike's vision.

A murderer's eyes were transplanted into the body of a law-abiding citizen. Now what determined the identity of those eyes? Suppose this scenario: A friend of Mike comes up and says, "Hey, Mike, how are you? You're looking great...except..." He leans closer, squints, and exclaims in horror, "Do you realize that you have a murderer's eyes?

"How silly!" you would say, and you would be right. The character or behavior of the person who looked through those eyes before is absolutely of no account now. The eyes now belong to Mike. Those eyes take on the identity of the person in whom they live. Like the "murderer's eyes" that were transplanted into the body of another man, the Bible teaches that every Christian has been "transplanted" into Jesus Christ (Romans 6:3-4). It no longer matters where he was; his identity is now "in Christ."

I am in Christ, as Noah and his family were in the ark, and thus I am saved from the avenging flood of God's wrath against sin, for Jesus is the Ark upon whom the flood of righteous indignation against sin has fallen. In Him I am safe, because He has borne the judgment for me. Indeed, I have borne the judgment, in Him!

I am in Christ, as the children of Israel were in the blood-sprinkled houses on the night of the Passover, and thus I am delivered from the darkness and eternal death of sin. Jesus is the Lamb whose blood was shed for me, and this blood, applied by faith to my heart, provides salvation and security to me.

I am in Christ, as the unintentional man-slayer who fled to the city of refuge was saved from the avenger, and was safe till the death of the high priest, if he abode in the refuge (Numbers 35:25-28). Jesus, our great High Priest, will never die, for He lives in the power of an endless life. Thus, He saves to the uttermost (Hebrews 7:25), for He is the "Author of eternal salvation unto all them that obey Him" (Hebrews 5:9). The avenger of the broken law cannot touch me, because I am in Him.

One Christian friend said to another, "How blessed it is to be 'safe in the arms of Jesus!'" "Yes," the friend replied, "but, my brother, we are safer than that." "Safer than that!" replied the first friend in astonishment. "How much safer can you be?" The friend replied, "My brother, we are as safe as an arm of Jesus!" It seems hard for some Christians to grasp, but the truth is that a Christian is as safe, as secure, and as well-supplied before God as Christ Himself! As a Christian, my residence is in Christ, my resources are in Christ, and my responsibility (to abide) is in Christ. The place of my PRIMARY ENVIRONMENT is in Christ.

MY PROGRESSIVE DEVELOPMENT — among "all the saints."

The place of the believer's *progressive development* is to be among the saints; that is, he is to grow and develop as a Christian in a fellowship of other Christians.

The place of the believer's progressive development is among "all the saints". In our earlier illustration, the traveler on the Queen Mary is not alone. He is traveling with a large number of fellow travelers. He is on a large "passenger list", and he is forced to adjust to the other passengers in the confines of the ship in which they are all traveling. He may find some of his traveling companions to be quite kindly, companionable and helpful. He may find others to be hateful, spiteful, and critical. And sometimes, the same travelers may shift from friendly to unfriendly while on the voyage!

Hopefully, fellow travelers would be strengthened and inspired by each other. Hopefully, they would find stimulus, encouragement, relationship, support and pleasure in each other.

However, realism forces us to admit that such hopes are not always realized when passengers are thrown together on the same voyage.

The illustration may be clearly seen by admitting that the Christian is inserted into a family the moment he is saved. He is immediately placed in an army with other soldiers. He is in a choir with other singers. This is seen in the text by examining the phrase, "all the saints." It is in the fellowship of the saints that the Christian is to develop. And the fellowship of the saints is an excellent laboratory for his development. Because of much abuse and misuse, the word "saints" is difficult to rescue today. According to the Bible, a saint is a sinner who has been "justified", or declared righteous or holy by God, even while he is apparently a long way from saintliness. A sinner does not become a saint by any performance or morality of his own, but solely through faith in Jesus Christ. God declares the believing sinner to be a saint on the basis of the perfection of Christ's Person and redeeming work on the Cross. At the moment of transfer of trust from self to Christ, God sees the redeemed sinner as being as perfect as Christ Himself. Having declared him a saint, God proceeds through the work of sanctification to make the saint saintly. This is a life-long process, and one of the important means God uses in this process is the total involvement the believer has in the church, the larger fellowship of "all the saints." It is of great importance that the word "saint" is almost always plural ("saints") in the Bible. Indeed, I think there is only one exception in the New Testament, and even there, it is plural in concept ("every saint"). The eight occurrences of the word in the book of Philippians are all plural.

So the Christian is a person who is learning to live in the plural, making whatever adjustments are necessary to live with other saints, even when they are very objectionable! These adjustments are growth mechanisms in the Christian life, even the very difficult ones. You see, as Christians, we are all the sheep of one flock, the branches of one vine, the brothers and sisters of one family, the children of one Father, the living stones of one building, the cells in one body. John Wesley was right when he said, "There is simply no such thing as a solitary Christian." Dr. William Clow said, "The truth is, that faith in Christ cannot be maintained without the fellowship of His people. The Christian life cannot survive without common prayer, common song, common worship. It thrives only by the ministry of the Word and the partnership of worship and service."

At the very inception of Christianity, Jesus began with a core of men, many of whom were already socially related. While He drew them into relationship with Himself, each was simultaneously being drawn into a relationship with every other member of the group. They occasionally competed with each other and argued among themselves, but this close-knit fellowship was the laboratory in which He fashioned them into world-impacting disciples. They were saints the moment Jesus called them and they began to follow Him, for the word simply means something or someone that God takes out of common use and puts to consecrated use, to His use. The word "holy," which is the root word for the word "saint", means separated and set aside. All Christians have been separated from a life of sin and common use and have been set apart unto Christ. And we can only "comprehend with all saints what is the breadth and length and depth and height of the love of Christ, which passes knowledge" (Ephesians 3:19).

If you as a Christian put environment number two (your place among the saints) before environment number one (your position in Christ), you will be a social, fellowshiping Christian, regular in church attendance, but with no reality or power at the core of your spiritual life. The life we enjoy in the church and among the saints must be a product of our position in Christ and our abiding in Him. After all, when two objects get close to a mutual or common third party, the closer they necessarily get to each other. And this relationship of each Christian with other Christians is the training ground for maturing each Christian in Christ and in the appointed ministry God has for him. The place of my *progressive development* is among the saints in the church of God.

MY PRACTICAL ASSIGNMENT — "at Philippi."

The place of the believer's *practical assignment* is "at Philippi." His first involvement for Christ is to be at his residence, in his neighborhood, in the community where he lives. In the New Testament, it might have been at Jerusalem, at Antioch, at Tarsus, at Ephesus, at Colossae, at Corinth, or at Rome. Today, it might be at Memphis, at St. Louis, at Little Rock, at Nashville, at Mobile, at Jacksonville, at Dallas — wherever the believer lives.

To return to our illustration, where you live corresponds to the ocean around the ship which the passenger is traveling on. The ocean transports the ship, but the ocean is a big problem to the ship. The world is the Christian's workshop, but it also provides a giant threat and a big challenge to the Christian. Jesus said that His followers are to be "in the world, but not of it." Our residence is in the world, but our primary resources are not to come from the world. You see, when a person is traveling across the ocean by ship, the ocean can be a test to the ship and a threat to the passenger.

A lady was in a briefing session with other prospective travelers before embarking on an ocean voyage. She said to the Captain, "Sir, what do we do if we get seasick?" He replied wryly, "Don't worry, Ma'am, you'll do it!" And she did get seasick on the voyage. She was leaning over the railing of the ship, "doing" the usual unpleasantry, when a man said to her, "Do you have a weak stomach, Ma'am?" "Weak, nothing!" she retorted, "I'm throwing it as far as anyone!" She was still there that evening when a romantic couple saw her. Associating her with their feelings, the young man said, "Are you waiting for the moon to come up?" She replied forlornly, *"Oh, no! Does that have to come up, too?"* An ocean voyage can be pleasant or uncomfortable, depending on the passenger's adjustment to his ocean environment.

The environment of this world can be a Christian's greatest obstacle. "Philippi" was a pagan outpost of Rome, a Roman colony, with its "far side" facing out onto heathen barbarism. So it was a center of anti-God philosophy and activity. It was here that God established through the Apostle Paul the first Christian work in Europe. And it was here that the first European Christians — Lydia, the converted slave-girl, the converted Philippian jailer, and other new believers were required to "flesh out" their relationship with Christ. Their most unfavorable atmosphere was this godless world, seen in the text in the term, "at Philippi." Charles Erdman wrote, "It is imperative that Christians constantly remind themselves that spiritual states do not depend upon physical surroundings or conditions." How true! We may live in a floodtide of iniquity, of blasphemy, of unbelief, of spiritual scorn and ridicule, of secularism and materialism, but it will never bother us as long as it does not get inside of us. That statement fits our analogy of the ship and the ocean. The place for a ship is in the ocean, but pity the people on board if the ocean gets in the ship! The Christian's place of service is in the world, but pity him and the ones he should minister to if the world gets in the Christian. So the Bible says, "Love not the world, neither the things that are in the world, for if any man love the world, the love for the Father is not in him." You see, if you allow environment number three (your place in this alien world) to take precedence over environments numbers one or two, if you put Philippi before your position in Christ or your fellowship with other believers, you will be a worldly Christian, and your effectiveness for Christ will disappear. But I have a reassuring word for the weak, or wavering, or wondering child of God: take proper care of the first two environments, and this third one will never be able to beat you down.

The more a Christian grows up in Christ, the more he will see the world as his opportunity. What am I to do with regard to this unbelieving world? I am to fill my outermost environment (the world) with my innermost environment (Christ). So my life becomes a vocation of adjustment (abiding in Christ and in fellowship with other believers) and re-adjustment (restoring fellowship with Christ and other Christians when that fellowship is broken).

Some years ago, a tragic air crash took from our world a great civil servant. He was Dag Hammarskjold, the late Secretary-General of the United Nations. Mr. Hammarskjold would probably not be recognized as an orthodox Christian, but when he died, he had with him a well-marked copy of Thomas a Kempis' Imitation of Christ. Mr. Hammarskjold's life, from all accounts, reflected much of the mind of Christ. He was a man who was immersed in international politics and the resolution of deeply-entrenched social problems. But running parallel to this public life was a private one, an interior life of uncommon richness. Though he was courageously involved in this world, he was also at home in another world, the world of the quiet spirit. In daily contact with man, he passionately sought prayerful communion with God. In his book entitled *Markings*, he wrote this powerful sentence: "The road to holiness always passes necessarily through the world of action." James, the half-brother of Jesus, made the same statement when he commanded, "Be ye doers of the word, and not hearers only."

George Fox said, "The world should be full of little bright lights wherever Christians are." Every Philippi on earth should have a landscape dotted with such lights.

Bring yourself under judgment right now. Are you sensible about environment number one? Are you sensitive to environment number two? Are you serving in environment number three? There is one more environment for a Christian. It is often ignored and misunderstood, but Christ's Great Commission cannot be fulfilled until this environment is understood and exploited as He commanded. This environment concerns the greatest vocation in the Christian life, that of being a disciple and building other disciples as Jesus commanded.

MY PERSONAL INVESTMENT AND FULFILLMENT — "Paul and Timothy."

The place of the believer's greatest *personal investment* and his greatest personal fulfillment is suggested by the opening phrase of this epistle, "Paul and Timothy." This little phrase opens up an entire universe of relationship, discipleship, fulfillment, and destiny.

Let's "circle" awhile before we solidly "land" on this point. It is a law in the life of a child of God that there is no success without successors. This is the way the purpose of God is advanced from generation to generation. The success of God's purpose is always assured (if at all) by the presence of a legal successor to the original contract, just as in our law, in which a contract is binding upon "heirs, successors, and assigns." Look, for example, at the story of Abraham in the Bible. The covenant God established with Abraham is never mentioned without reference to Abraham's descendants, his "seed," his successor or successors. Now, press the "Fast Forward" key and move all the way to the time of Jesus. The slaughter of baby boys in Judea after Christ's birth by Herod the Roman puppet-king, was an attempt (just one of many) to destroy God's genetic line to Abraham's ultimate successor, Jesus. And even Jesus, the Ultimate Successor, left a successor — the Holy Spirit.

Looking back again into history, we remember that Moses left a successor in Joshua. But Joshua left no successor. So the Jewish people were not strong enough for many years to control the land and live in peace. They were finally led (erratically) by an irregular series of "judges," like Samson, to battle with the Philistines. The first Jewish king was Saul, and he left no successor. He was Divinely displaced by David, who left a succession of kings to rule the land, starting with Solomon. So we see the strong suggestion that a man could neither live nor die successfully without a successor.

We are all familiar with the sad picture of a "winner-take-all" achievement, a solitary conquest meant to be enjoyed and celebrated only by the victor, whose personal satisfaction is his only aim in life. The entertainment media makes this a frequent plot premise, presenting a "lone ranger" as hero or anti-hero who lives for the moment. However, the Bible presents us with a distinctively different standard, that of success through a successor. This is the standard of multiplicative disciple-making in the New Testament, the standard Jesus masterfully followed in building twelve men who would be entrusted with the transformation of the world. Dietrich Bonhoeffer said, "The truly righteous man is the man who lives for the next generation." E. Stanley Jones wrote, "The wise man is the man who plants a tree under whose shade he knows he will never sit." The Divine genius of Christianity is clearly seen in the three stark words, "Paul and Timothy." The Bible does offer a "success standard," though it is admittedly strange in the world's eyes. In the Bible, no achievement is ever legitimately made merely in one's own name. Often the "success" God works through us does far more for others than for ourselves.

One of the most renowned names in the game of golf is that of Harvey Penick. His name never appeared on a winner's trophy at a PGA golf tournament, but when Penick died at the age of 90, the world of golf lost one of its greatest teachers. Although his books have sold millions of copies (and the publication of them almost never occurred, because of his modesty), he was remembered most for his direct impact on people. An Associated Press story stated, "Penick refused to teach methods or group lessons, instead applying his wisdom to the talents of individual players." Tom Kite, the leading money winner in PGA Tour history, was 13 when he began working with Penick. Ben Crenshaw began learning the game from Penick at the age of 6. Any golf fan of today will have etched on his memory the picture of Crenshaw on his knees on the eighteenth green of Augusta National Golf Course after sinking the winning putt in the 1995 Masters Golf Tournament. Crenshaw was in tears, and he stated that his week at the Masters was emotionally wrenching to him, not merely because of the pressure of tournament competition, but also because his lifelong teacher, Harvey Penick, had died that week. Penick, who could have spent his life speaking to crowds, chose instead to invest himself in individual persons — many of them children — one at a time.

The Apostle Paul modeled this kind of unselfish discipling, or mentoring with a mission, with a young man named Timothy. Then he urged Timothy to do the same with others. He wrote, "The things that you have heard from me...commit these to faithful men who will be able to teach others also" (II Timothy 2:2).

"Paul and Timothy." Here we see the importance of one disciple (nobody can have two until he first has one). If we really operated in a Christ-like manner and by His method, would there be any single specific work that would always characterize us? Yes! Jesus clearly modeled the strategy which He mandated in the Great Commission, and both model and mandate are exemplified in the words, "Paul and Timothy."

The Commission of Jesus is to "turn people into disciples," and His own method and ministry provide the only acceptable interpretation of His command. Every Christian is commanded to "turn people into disciples," and this must be done reasonably after the model of Jesus if it is to be done properly. One of my most important environments is the small atmosphere which prevails around me and my disciple. One of my most important involvements is my involvement with my disciple. The procedure and product of my disciple-making ministry must be constantly measured by those of Jesus, so the final test is in the product. I cannot succeed without a successor, a disciple. Pastor Rick Yohn said, "I developed a boldness for witnessing by following the example of one man. I developed a consistent prayer life by following the example of another." The principle of succession is an indispensable principle in true Christianity.

Paul was simply following the command of Jesus when he won and trained Timothy, his disciple. Thus Paul was a very wise man. He decided that the best way to strengthen and maximize his own ministry was to pour his life into others, and then multiply himself through them. So he made a conscious choice to restrict his other ministries as much as was necessary to stake his own future productivity on the faithful ministry of Timothy and other disciples whom he also trained. Certain names are highlighted in the New Testament simply because Paul discipled them, names such as Silas, John Mark, Trophimus, Tychicus, Aquila, Priscilla, Titus, and Luke. Two casualties came from that group — John Mark, a part-time casualty who later recovered (through the ministry of another disciple-maker, Barnabas!) and wrote the Gospel of Mark. The other casualty, Demas, apparently never recovered from his defection. Remember that even Jesus had a "rotten egg" in His Dozen!

"Paul and Timothy." This uniting of names and personalities and service also reveals the importance of teamwork in the world-impacting plan of God. Something about Timothy's presence provided great encouragement to Paul. Every disciple-maker knows what that "something" was. And surely Paul encouraged Timothy as well. In Exodus 17 is the story of a battle between the children of Israel and the Amalekites. It was a strange battle. Joshua was the general, fighting at the battlefront. Moses was on the top of a nearby hill with the rod of God in his hand. But two other men were also involved, Aaron and Hur. When Moses lifted up his hands, Joshua went forward; when Moses tired and dropped his hands, Joshua retreated. That's when Aaron and Hur got into the act. They raised Moses' hands for him and the battle was won. Timothy and Silas may have played the roles of Aaron and Hur for Paul. They certainly kept Paul's hands lifted. Everyone knows about the Apostle Paul, just as everyone knows about Moses. But behind the scenes were Timothy and Silas and other team members, encouraging, supporting, facilitating, trouble-shooting, and engaging in shuttle diplomacy. As a result, great spiritual battles were won. And prayer support is only one of the group dynamics which may be used to advantage in a team model. A team milieu provides a sense of belonging and security, facilitates opportune mutual encouragement, permits vocational stimulation and accountability, and allows the exchange of hands-on challenge. "Iron sharpens iron" — and though sparks may fly from the friction of the encounter, weapons are fashioned which God may choose to deploy for infinite purposes. May He be pleased to do so with us!

The Christian is provided with an advance agenda for functioning in all four "environments" or "worlds" in which he lives. He is responsible to abide in Christ (John 15:4). He is responsible to impact the world for Christ's sake, both locally and globally (Acts 1:8). He is responsible to love the saints (John 15:12). And he is responsible to "turn people into disciples" (Matthew 28:19) to enlarge Christ's influence to the ends of the earth until the end of time. Christian, are you living in all four worlds? Are you exercising yourself effectively in all four environments? Are you consistently abiding in Christ? Are you enjoying the company and experiencing the crucible of the fellowship of believers? Are you exerting a positive influence for the Savior in your Phillipi? Are you discipling some Timothy for total world impact?

Chapter 2

Looking into the Heart of a Disciple-Maker

Paul and Timothy, bond-servants of Christ Jesus, the Messiah, to all the saints (God's consecrated people) in Christ Jesus who are at Philippi, with the bishops (overseers) and deacons (assistants): Grace (favor and blessing) to you and heart peace from God our Father and the Lord Jesus Christ, the Messiah. I thank my God in all my remembrance of you. In every prayer of mine I always make my entreaty and petition for you all with joy (delight). (I thank my God) for your fellowship — your sympathetic co-operation and contributions and partnership — in advancing the good news (the Gospel) from the first day (you heard it) until now. And I am convinced and sure of this very thing, that He Who began a good work in you will continue until the day of Jesus Christ — right up to the time of His return — developing (that good work) and perfecting and bringing it to full completion in you. It is right and appropriate for me to have this confidence and feel this way about you all, because even as you do me, I hold you in my heart as partakers and sharers, one and all with me, of grace (God's unmerited favor and spiritual blessing). (This is true) both when I am shut up in prison and when I am out in the defense and confirmation of the good news (the Gospel). For God is my witness how I long for and pursue you all with love, in the tender mercies of Christ Jesus (Himself)! (Philippians 1:1-8, Amplified Bible)

Have you ever accidentally come across a box of old letters in an attic? Multiplied millions of such letters must be stored in attics and closets around the world. I have in my library several volumes of letters written by renowned people. Some of them comprise very insightful and valuable reading to a Christian. However, none of them can match the importance of an old letter written by an old missionary nearly 2000 years ago, and kept in the old library of letters and books which we call the Bible. The old letter is a brief epistle written by the aging apostle Paul to a growing fellowship of Christian believers in the Roman colony of Philippi in what we now recognize as southern Europe. The letter to the Philippians is perhaps the greatest pastoral document ever written. Because it was written by a skilled disciple-maker, its purpose was to make and mature Christian disciples.

Our Bible has been divided into chapters and verses for our convenience in reading and studying it. However, we must remember that the epistle to the Philippians was a personal letter, and was not divided into such units. If we can imagine it handwritten and occupying the page like a letter, we may better get the feel of its message. Let me encourage you to read the above passage in at least two other good translations of the New Testament before you go further in this study.

One of the most serious mistakes we make in Bible study is to suppose that we know what is in a book, or chapter, or paragraph, or sentence of Scripture just because we have previously read it. The experience of multitudes of Bible students through the centuries is entirely to the contrary. The vast hidden wealth of the Word of God is such that new light may break forth from its pages after years of frequent meditation and familiar acquaintance. To have read it previously may be only to know its structure, its outer form of words, what it says on the surface. We say that we "know" a man when we first meet him. In reality, however, we hardly know him at all, only his name, form, appearance, and a few outer mannerisms. His wife, after years of intimacy with him, may truly affirm that she knows him — and even then there are hidden provinces in his character that are probably more vast than the little she knows! Please re-read this passage several times more. Repetitive reading may develop in each of us a greater capacity for seeing more of the truth that is here. Also, it will teach you directly more and more how to feed yourself from Scripture instead of being fed from someone else's spoon.

THE GREAT GREETING THAT PAUL EXTENDED

Paul's greeting to the Philippians follows the usual style of a first-century letter. It includes an identification of the sender or senders, the subjects, and a salutation (verses 1-2). The senders are "Paul and Timothy," though Timothy is not a co-writer of the letter. Note all the personal pronouns that refer to Paul alone, and the mention of Timothy as a separate person. Timothy is included because of his association with Paul, and that association included a relationship with the Philippian church. The subjects or recipients of the letter are "all the saints at Philippi."

Then comes the salutation. It is impossible to over-estimate the importance of these words: "Grace and peace to you from God our Father and the Lord Jesus Christ." In this salutation, we see: the grace that is responsible for our salvation and sanctification, the peace that is the all-inclusive result of our salvation, and the source from which this grace and peace are released. So we want to examine the summary words, "grace and peace," the sequence in which those words occur, and the source from which those benefits come.

"Grace to you." Can we possibly grasp the meaning and magnitude of the word "grace"? It is properly called "amazing grace," but amazing grace is a "Him", and not just a hymn. The word "grace" occurs 156 times in the New Testament (100 times in Paul's letters), and is the overwhelming short-hand word for all that God does for sinful human beings.

In his book <u>Lion and Lamb,</u> Brennan Manning wrote, "Unfortunately, the whole concept of grace is alien to the American psyche. In our culture the tradition of 'rugged individualism' has assumed a religious dimension. Americans are the people par excellence who get things done. Give us enough time, money, and manpower and we can achieve anything. Listen to all the Sunday sermons with their emphasis on will-power and personal effort, and you get the impression that a do-it-yourself spirituality is the American fashion, that the Pelagian heresy of salvation that is completed by self-effort is very much in vogue. Though the Scriptures speak insistently of the Divine initiative in the work of salvation, that by grace we are saved, that the Tremendous Lover has taken to the chase, American spirituality still seems to start with self, not with God. Personal responsibility replaces personal response. We seem engrossed in producing our own salvation and in our own efforts to grow in holiness. The emphasis is always more on what I do rather than on what God is doing in my life. In this macho approach God is reduced to a benign old spectator on the sidelines. We have convinced ourselves that we can do a pretty good job of following Jesus if we just, once and for all, make up our minds and really buckle down to it."

In contrast to the vain self-flattery of sinners seeking to accomplish their own salvation, the Bible gives a ringing cry throughout its pages that salvation, sanctification, and service are all of grace. Malcolm Muggeridge expressed the Christian view when he wrote, "Christianity is not a statistical view of life. That there should be more joy in heaven over one sinner who repents than over all the hosts of the just, is an anti-statistical proposition." Think carefully here. When Jesus originally made the statement about the "one sinner who repents" and the "ninety and nine just persons who need no repentance" (Luke 15:7, at the conclusion of the story of the lost sheep), it seems that the word "just" refers to people who think they are just, but really are not. Blaise Pascal, the French mathematician and philosopher, said, "There are actually only two kinds of people in the world, those who think themselves to be righteous, but aren't, and those who know themselves to be sinners, but aren't reckoned so by God — they are justified by His grace." There's that word again!

Just what is grace? An unknown author wrote, "Henry Wadsworth Longfellow could write a poem worth hundreds of dollars, and we call that talent. John Jacob Astor could sign his name to a piece of paper, buy a skyscraper, and we call that wealth. The United States Treasury Department can take a special piece of paper and some special ink, press it between special plates, make a $100 bill, and we call that money. The Wright Brothers took some used bicycle parts, wire, metal and canvas covering, made an airplane, and we call that genius. Michelangelo could take some brushes and some paints and paint a masterpiece on the ceiling of the Sistine Chapel, and we call that art. A mechanic can take a used and ruined part from your automobile engine, replace it with a new one, make the car nearly as good as new, and we call that skill. And God can take a poor, worthless, devastated, hell-bound sinner, wash him clean in the blood of Jesus Christ, place His Holy Spirit in him, transform him into a brand new person — and we call that GRACE!" But what is grace?

Grace is the free, spontaneous, unmerited love of God to sinful man, a love that has been manifested in human experience and reached its highest expression in "the redemption that is in Christ Jesus" (Romans 3:24). But it is exactly at this point that man's problem lies. The last thing we wretched humans desire and learn is to be the recipients of unearned, unattained, blood-bought Divine favor, through the sovereign will of God: objects merely of grace. Repeat it over and over. We are not saved and kept by our goodness, but by His grace; not by our merit, but by His mercy; not by our performance, but by His power. Grace has reference to what God is and does, not to what we are and do. Grace supposes all the sin and evil that is in us, and takes all of our sins (past, present, and future) into consideration before it acts. Our supposed goodness contributes nothing to our salvation, and our obvious sinfulness does not prevent salvation. To think that any contribution of goodness or any correction of sin on our part can get us into a saving relationship with God is to put ourselves into competition with Jesus Christ.

Can you imagine going to God after you have lived your life and saying, "Now Lord, I didn't exactly fit into that grace category. But I have lived a good life, and I appeal to my good life." No matter how fully we recite and rehearse our supposed virtues before Him, I would guess that God would reply in some fashion like this: "What do you think the infinite cross of My Son was all about? Why do you think I sent Jesus into the world if you could have done it yourself? Nothing you could do would satisfy Me, because you are a sinner. But My precious Son and His Death have fully satisfied Me. Your offer to pay for your salvation by contribution or correction is the infinite insult against My Darling Son and His infinite Death on the Cross." You see, anything in my salvation that I had the smallest possible right to expect could not be pure, free grace. It is all of grace! The commencement, continuation, and consummation of salvation are all of grace. F. B. Meyer was right when he said that "this marvelous word is aglow with heaven's altar flame." Grace permits us to come to God as empty sinners to be saved and blessed, empty of right feelings, good character, and satisfactory record, with nothing to commend us but our deep need, fully and frankly acknowledged. This concept will always be absurd to the unaided human mind. In fact, the only thing more absurd than the gift of grace is our stubborn refusal to receive it.

Perhaps grace is better presented in pictures than in abstract words. Dr. Roy Angell relates a story of pastor S. M. Lindsay before he came to America. At the time, he taught a class of boys in a Sunday School in Scotland. One day according to Lindsay, he was walking down an icy street to attend an afternoon tea. He was dressed in a high top hat, striped trousers, a cutaway coat, and spats. As he walked along the icy street, he saw Bobby, one of his Sunday School boys, lurking behind one of the bushes lining the street. Suddenly, without warning, an ice ball hit Lindsay on the side of the head, knocking his silk hat into the mud and causing Lindsay to see stars. He knew young Bobby was the culprit. He went on to the tea wondering how he should respond to Bobby's mischief. And he decided that he would return good for evil. Remembering that he had loaned his three-part fishing pole to Bobby a few days earlier, Lindsay went to the hardware store and bought another pole. Taking it to Bobby's house, he knocked at the door and asked if Bobby were home. "Yes," Bobby's mother replied as she called Bobby. But Bobby didn't respond. He had gone out the back door when he saw his Sunday School teacher walking up to the front door. Lindsay told Bobby's mother to give him the fishing pole and to tell him that his Sunday School teacher wanted him to have it. And he added, "Tell him I know he needs it." A couple of hours later there was a timid knock at Lindsay's door. Opening the door, Lindsay saw Bobby sheepishly standing there with the fishing pole in hand. "Mr. Lindsay," Bobby said quietly, "I'm returning your fishing pole. I need it, but I don't deserve it." "Bobby," Mr. Lindsay said, "what was our Sunday School lesson about last Sunday?" "I don't remember," said Bobby timidly. "Sure you do, Bobby. Don't you remember that it was a lesson about God's grace? And what did I tell you about God's grace?" Bobby's eyes brightened as he answered, "Oh, I remember now. You told us that grace is something we need but don't deserve."

"Exactly," said Mr. Lindsay. "And that's why I want you to keep the gift. I knew you didn't deserve it when I gave it to you." God's grace is like that. It is something we desperately need, but do not in any way deserve. Someone wisely said, "Grace is God doing for us what we could not possibly do for ourselves — and charging us nothing for it."

> *When I was a child and had nothing to pay*
> *They fed me and clothed me, day upon day,*
> *She nursed me in measles and other such ills*
> *And mended my clothes, and he paid the bills.*
> *They hoped, and feared, and prayed for me too*
> *And saved me from evil and carried me through*
> *I never knew how, and I never knew why*
> *They should wear out their lives for a thing such as I.*
> *Well, that was just their way.*
> *I was a child and had nothing to pay.*
> *Those days are far gone: I grew to a man*

> *A respectable person according to plan*
> *Took sixteen in collars and wore a black coat*
> *Political candidates called for my vote.*
> *I wrote to the papers and gave them my views*
> *Preached to the people all patient in pews*
> *I was paid once a month and had a bank account*
> *With a checkbook thrown in to show the amount.*
> *Was it worth all God's trouble?*
> *So much of my life is wood, hay, stubble*
> *So little is good that could meet His desire*
> *So much of me bad, only fit for the fire.*
> *If God calls for a reckoning, Ah! What shall I say?*
> *"Lord, this poor sinner has nothing to pay.."*
> *"Nothing to pay! Give him justice," they say.*
> *"Nothing for nothing! Take him away!"*
> *But God says, "Stay!*
> *Christ is just for those who have nothing to pay."*
> *Remember, helpless sinner, that is God's way,*
> *Christ is for those who have nothing to pay!*

Grace is the beginning point for our original salvation ("by grace are you saved"), and grace provides the ongoing supply ("God is able to make all grace abound toward you") for the continuation and completion of the Christian life. When I think of grace, I remember the account of the old lady who made her first trip to the seashore. She gazed for a few minutes at the vast expanse of water, then she said, "Thank God for something there is enough of!"

"Peace", the second blessing in Paul's benediction, is the effect of the activation of grace in a person's life. Grace is the root of all of God's redemptive action in our lives, and peace is the fruit of it. "Grace and peace" are inseparable. They are mutually inclusive. They are the "Siamese twins" of salvation. So, having discussed grace, we now examine its traveling companion, "peace." Man is not naturally at peace with God. By nature, man is at war with God, either passively or actively, and being at war with God we are also at war with each other and at war with ourselves. That is why there is so much misery and unrest in the world. But God gives peace when his grace reigns in a human life, and it is this peace that Paul includes in his benediction to the Philippian believers.

Three kinds of peace are clearly distinguishable in Scripture. One is *peace with God*, which comes when we are reconciled to God by trusting Jesus Christ as Lord and Savior. One is *the peace of God*, which prevails in the believer as he surrenders himself totally to Christ without reserve or regret. And one is peace between men. Proverbs 16:7 says that "when a man's ways are pleasing to the Lord, He makes even his enemies to be at peace with him." Peace with God is the peace which He gives to a sinner when he trusts Christ. The peace of God is the peace which He is in the life of a saint. Peace among men is much harder to attain, because so many of our associates are lost people who do not have peace with God, and many are saved people who may not have "the peace of God, which passes understanding, standing guard over their hearts and minds in Christ Jesus" (Philippians 4:7). So the word peace has upward, inward and outward dimensions to it. Stated negatively, man is not at peace with his fellow man because he is not at peace with himself, and man is not at peace with himself because he is not at peace with God. Peace with God is God's gracious gift to the unbeliever who repents of sin and trusts Jesus as Savior and Lord. The peace of God is God's gracious gift to the faith-walking believer. Hopefully, then, the peace of God will continually prevail in the life of that believer.

People in whom the peace of God reigns are like a clock in a thunderstorm. There may be outside turbulence all around, but the clock just keeps on moving at the manufacturer's pace! Someone asked a boy on a train, "Where are you going?" He replied, "I don't know." "You don't know! Well, aren't you afraid?" "No, because my Daddy is the engineer on this train." "Thou wilt keep him in perfect peace whose mind is stayed (stopped) on Thee" (Isaiah 26:3).

Now notice the connection of the two benedictory words, "grace and peace." This sequence always prevails, and it cannot be violated. "Get grace and all gifts are gained. Grace is the bountiful mother of all the graces," said John Henry Jowett. And peace is the summary word for all the benefits which enter our lives through grace. Where grace abides peace will prevail. But grace will always precede peace. You may search Scripture through and through for an exception, but you will never find peace mentioned first when the two are associated. It is always "grace and peace," never "peace and grace." No human being will ever have true peace until he has received the grace of God, and he will never have grace until he has received Christ. Grace and peace is the Divine order of the two blessings. In the Old Testament sacrificial system the sin offering had to precede the peace offering, and here the same sequence is followed. Grace must do its work in a sinner's heart before there can be any peace there. Incidentally, when a peace-offering was made, a part of it was burned up. In the typology of the Old Testament, this signifies that God was satisfied. A part went to the priest, signifying that Christ was satisfied. And part was eaten by the offerer, showing that the sinner was satisfied. The peace of God is a most satisfying blessing!

Eric Barker was an English missionary who served more than fifty years in Portugal. During World War II, life in Portugal became so dangerous that Barker was advised to send his wife and eight children to England for safety. His sister and her three children were also evacuated on the same ship. Barker remained behind to conclude some missionary matters. When he stood to preach the next Sunday morning, he told his congregation he had just received news that his family had safely arrived home. It was not until later that the congregation understood what Barker meant. They thought he meant his family was safe in England, but that wasn't the case. Just before he went into the pulpit to preach that Sunday morning, he had been handed a telegram telling him that a German submarine had torpedoed the ship on which his family was sailing. All passengers had perished. They had arrived safely home, not to England, but to heaven where Jesus had welcomed them! This peace is our legacy, our privilege to have. Jesus is our peace (Ephesians 2:14), and circumstances must not control us.

Just as we tried to define grace, we must now seek to define peace. Peace has two sides to it. One side is the absence of warfare; the other side is the prevalence of welfare. Peace is not the absence of movement; it is rather the absence of friction. The best symbol of peace is not a placid and motionless mountain lake, but rather the smooth flow of a vast river. Peace is not best pictured in a death chamber, but in the rhythmic movements of a great engine. The Greek word translated "peace" is the word *eirene*, which means "to bind together." Outside of Christ, everything tends to be diseased and disjointed.

Hamlet said, "The times are out of joint," and the same thing can be said about human hearts in which Christ does not live. They are naturally characterized by discord, agitation, conflict, and strife. But when grace reaches the heart, when Christ is within, a harmonized relationship is established — upward, inward, and outward. Grace and peace are never reversed in expression in the Bible, and they are never reversed in experience in the believer.

Then Paul's benedictory statement identifies the source of grace and peace. "Grace to you and peace from God our Father and the Lord Jesus Christ." God the Father may be regarded as the source from which these blessings come, and Jesus His Son may be regarded as the medium through which they come. These blessings cannot come from the world, or from our circumstances, or from our independent inner being, but only from God through Christ. The Father and the Son have an absolute monopoly on the gifts of grace and peace, and they cannot be obtained from any other source. Jowett said, "The river of grace and peace has its rise in the vast, two-sphered, and yet indivisible lake of 'God our Father and the Lord Jesus Christ.' 'Every good and perfect gift is from above,' and away to this lofty spring the Apostle traces the river of 'grace and peace.' And let us carefully heed how firmly and naturally the Apostle exalts the Lord Jesus to the supreme rank of Divine Sovereignty. The Lord Jesus is one with the Father in the holy initiative of redeeming grace. He shares with the Father the glory of all redeeming ministries, and is one with Him in the origin and sustenance of our salvation. 'From God our Father and the Lord Jesus Christ.'"

But we must give careful heed to the two relational words in this prepositional phrase, the words "Father" and "Lord." The source of all blessings is in God, but they can only come to us when God is our Father and Jesus Christ is our Lord. Is God your Father by a very real Divine birth? Is Jesus Christ your Lord by a very real acknowledgment of faith?

Remember that we are looking into a disciple-maker's heart. A disciple-maker's heart will be dominated by God, by the Lord Jesus Christ, by grace and peace, and by other people. His thoughts will often sound like the expressions of this opening section of the book of Philippians. Do you have a disciple-maker's heart? Come back again and again to this opening salutation and let God teach its great lessons to your soul.

THE GREAT GRATITUDE THAT PAUL EXPRESSED

One cannot read this paragraph of Paul's letter without detecting how incredibly relational it is. For this much warmth and depth to translate across that much time and distance is a miracle. The Apostle Paul may well have been as relational as any mere mortal who ever lived. A broad profile of his life as revealed in Scripture, as well as a "dip" into any of his writings, will reveal this. Our text is a case in point. How personal his words are! In a "book" of just four brief chapters, Paul uses the personal pronouns, "I," "me," and "my" over 100 times. The word "I" alone occurs 52 times. It would be easy to deduce from those statistics that Paul was a top-drawer egotist, but rather, the focus of his attention is on his readers, his brothers and sisters and friends and disciples in Philippi. Though Paul had a remarkably rich inner life, he lived an "inside-out" life, with the focus on Christ and others! Someone wisely said, "No one should be considered a Christian unless he considers the rights of others before his own feelings, and the feelings of others before his own rights." That would indeed provide a good practical test for one's profession as a Christian. True relational living requires a combination of genuine spirituality, inner serenity and security, an unselfish disposition, basic intelligence and emotional control. As to its interpersonal dimension, it requires a longing and a lingering to discover other people. Paul had these characteristics — and many more — in abundance.

Now, reread this text again several times, noting in one reading how positive his words are, then on the next reading note how passionate his words are, then on the next reading note how plain and straightforward they are. This was a large-hearted, people-oriented, faith-driven, Christ-controlled kind of man. Both his thoughts and his thanksgiving reveal how relational he was. Observe the sentence, "I thank my God upon every remembrance of you." Paul had known these friends somewhere between ten and twelve years. What an inventory of memories he would have! And yet he declares that he is able to thank God for every memory he has of them! He could not locate even one dark spot in the whole field on which the eye of memory rested. What a testimonial this is to Paul's tastes and thinking! A vulture will circle looking for death and rottenness, and will find it. But a honey bee circles looking for sweetness — and finds it. Paul's appetite determined that he would find sweetness in his friends and disciples. And what a testimonial it is to the faith of his readers! Let me interrupt our study with two practical questions: (l) What kind of memories do other people have when they think of me? (2) Am I personally engaging in activities and relationships that will store my memory bank with treasures instead of trinkets or trash?

It is obvious that many have lost the grace of gratitude today. There is a real talent within us for taking everything for granted. Should not more of our thoughts and words begin with the phrase, "I thank"? How often do you give thanks to God? Do you remember when Jesus healed ten lepers and only one came back with a semblance of thanksgiving? He said, "Were there not ten, and where are the nine?" We must remember to say proper thanksgiving for others before God, and to them face to face. The Christian who is eager in praise to God is not swift in the criticism of men. Paul was quick in expressing eulogies about men only because he was quicker in expressing doxologies to God.

What, in particular, was Paul thankful for when he looked over his memories of these Philippian brothers and sisters? He was thankful for their *fellowship in the Gospel* — verse five. The word "fellowship" is one of the gigantic words of the Gospel. It comes from a root word which means "commonness". You cannot have fellowship with other people unless you hold things in common with them. There are three great references to "fellowship" in the book of Philippians (1:5; 2:1; 3:10). We can detect four categories of fellowship in these three references. In 1:5, we see the fellowship of salvation and service. In 2:1, we see "fellowship in the Spirit," and in 3:10, we find "the fellowship of His sufferings." All of these fellowships introduce us into something very active, "the advance of the Gospel." Rich Christian fellowship requires a common faith, a common focus, and a common following of Christ. These things bound Paul and the Philippians believers together in a wonderful fellowship. You see, before they were saved, all Christians were participants in the same guilt. When they are saved, they become partakers of the same grace. And after they are saved, they become partners in the same Gospel.

Dr. John Townsend wrote this brilliant paragraph about fellowship. "In physics, the second law of thermodynamics is known as the law of entropy. It states that things that are isolated move toward deterioration. Entropy operates in the spiritual world too. Whatever is cut off tends toward deterioration. That's why the ultimate punishment, hell, is not defined by loss of consciousness or annihilation, but by its utter and complete separation from the love of God. That is why Jesus' sacrifice for us involved His own separation from the Father when He became sin on our behalf. He suffered in that 'He was cut off out of the land of the living' (Isaiah 53:8). In other words, there is no life without relationship."

Let's see if we can identify the ingredients of fellowship by examining this paragraph of Paul's Philippian letter. What bound the Philippian believers together?

First, they were all *professors of the same Lord.* Christ is referred to by name or pronoun six times in these verses, 18 times in chapter one, and 70 times in this brief letter! No wonder John Brown of Haddington exclaimed, "Paul writes as if Jesus were at his elbow!"

The Philippians were consolidated by faith in a common Lord. This is the first vital ingredient of fellowship.

Second, they were all *possessors of the same life*. In verse seven, Paul said, "You are all partakers with me of the grace of God." In verse six, he declares that God has done his "good work" of salvation in them. "We are confident of this very thing, that He who has begun a good work in you will perform it unto the day of Jesus Christ." What a salvation verse! Here we see the origination of salvation — "HE has begun a good work in you." And the initiation of salvation — it has been Divinely "BEGUN" in you. And the description of salvation — a "GOOD WORK". And the location of salvation —IN YOU". And the completion of salvation — "HE ... WILL COMPLETE IT." And the consummation of salvation — "UNTIL THE DAY OF JESUS CHRIST." Note again that salvation is a "good work" of God. Lost people struggle and fight against salvation as if it were an evil or bad work, but it is a good work. Salvation is good in origin, quality, purpose, and result. And this "good work" has been begun and is being carried to its conclusion in the Philippian Christians.

Third, they had all been *placed at the same level*. Grace is a great leveler! All Christians are partakers of the same life, and the grace of God places them together at the same level. This is a priceless truth, and it is clearly seen by examining the founding of the church at Philippi as recorded in Acts 16 (read this chapter carefully). The three first converts in Philippi were Lydia (a wealthy business woman), a demon-possessed slave girl, and a jailer. Lydia, though wealthy and prominent, did not receive a superior kind of spiritual life that was suited to her high social standing. Nor did the degraded, demented, demon-possessed slave girl get a kind of inferior quality of spiritual life suited to her social status! Nor did the jailer, a civil servant, get a different kind suited to him! The Christ they received was the same, the faith they exercised was the same, the grace they partook of was the same, the salvation they obtained was the same. No matter what distinctions may be made in society between men, they are all placed on the same level when they are saved.

Fourth, they were all *practitioners of the same love.* Paul expressed this love when he wrote to them, "I hold you in my heart" (vs. 7). And he extravagantly declared in verse eight, "God is my witness how greatly I long after you in the bowels of Jesus Christ." Apparently, real love is a "gutsy" thing! This seems to refer to the deep feeling inside a person which causes him to ache because he cares so much for another person. Paul said, "I hold you in my heart," not merely on my mind, or on my nerves, or on my lips. The proper place to carry disciples is in your heart, and the proper attitude toward them is one of love.

Amy Carmichael, the great missionary to India, expressed this negatively in a letter to her friends in the Dohnavur Fellowship: "Unlove is deadly. It is a cancer. It may kill slowly, but it always kills in the end. Let us fear it, fear to give room to it as we should fear to nurse a cobra. It is deadlier than any cobra. One drop of the gall of unlove in my heart or yours, however unseen, has a terrible power of spreading all through our Family, for we are one body — we are parts of one another. If one member suffers loss, all suffer loss. Not one of us liveth to himself. If unlove be discovered anywhere, stop everything and put it right, if possible, at once."

The love of Christ should motivate all the relationships that believers have with each other. When you received the life of Christ, you received the love of Christ. When His life came into you, His love came, too. You cannot separate the two. Romans 5:5 describes the experience of every Christian when it says, "The love of God is shed abroad in our hearts by the Holy Spirit who is given unto us." Paul simply echoed this experience when he wrote, "I hold you in my heart" — everywhere I go, I carry you around with me, as I think of you, love you, and pray for you. This is a clear look into a disciple-maker's heart.

Fifth, they were all *pursuers of the same longing.* They longed to see the Gospel advance, both locally and globally. Jesus said, "When the process (of disciple-making) is completed, the disciple will be like his teacher" (Luke 6:40). The Philippian disciples were a reflection of Paul, their disciple-maker. Because he had the world on his heart, so did they. They were partners together "in advancing the Gospel" (vs. 5). And he declared in verse 7, "You are partakers and sharers with me ... in the defense and confirmation of the Gospel." Note the words "defense and confirmation." These two terms are often used as legal terms, and they may describe Paul's trial before the imperial court of Rome. The word "defense" is used in II Timothy 4:16: "At my first defense no one supported me, but all deserted me." The words "defense and confirmation" describe the answer he gave to those who had brought charges against him which caused him to be in prison at this time. These words are now used to describe the work of advancing the Gospel. What do they mean? The word "defense" is more of a negative word, the word for giving arguments for removing doubts and suspicions. That is, this work is necessary to clear the ground for positive Gospel presentation. The entire life of every Christian should be an "apologia" (the Greek word for "defense") for the Gospel, removing difficulties, doubts and suspicions in preparation for the proclamation of the Gospel. And when necessary, the Christian should give a systematic doctrinal argument for the Gospel.

The very translation of the word "defense" suggests the action deals with a foe. However, the other word, "confirmation," carries the idea of strengthening, developing, and building up the friends of Jesus and the Gospel. This word certainly includes the disciple-making process. In fact, this is the very word that is used of Paul's activity in Asia Minor. Acts 14:21 says, " And they preached the Gospel to that city (Derbe), and taught (this is the verb form of the word "disciple") many, confirming the souls of the disciples." And the Philippian Christians were standing solidly with Paul in both activities, that of "defending" and that of "confirming" the Gospel. They were pursuers of a common longing.

With these ingredients of fellowship present in the church at Philippi, no wonder that Paul was grateful! Someone said, "If

Christians do no have the cement of true fellowship, they will fly apart from the centrifugal force of selfishness." May we be adhered together by "the tie that binds our hearts in Christian love," for "the fellowship of kindred minds is like to that fellowship which prevails above." Paul was thankful for the Philippians' fellowship in the Gospel.

He was thankful for their *faithfulness to the Gospel*. He wrote in verses five and six, "I thank my God for your fellowship — your sympathetic co-operation and contributions and partnership — in advancing the good news (the Gospel) from the first day (you heard it) until now. And I am convinced and sure of this very thing, that He Who began a good work in you will continue until the day of Jesus Christ --right up to the time of His return — developing (that good work) and perfecting and bringing it to full completion in you."

Note that Paul reminded them of that spectacular day in Philippi when the work of God began among them. He spoke of "the first day," the day when the Gospel came to town and God began His redemptive work there. This was the day when the Lord opened Lydia's heart to the Gospel, then she opened her home to the Gospel workers (Acts 16:14, 15). Then followed the conversions of the slave girl and the jailer (see Acts 16). Every work of God among men has a "first day." Every Christian has had a "first day." Every Christian life begins on a "first day." Paul himself was fond of repeating the story of his "first day" as a Christian (see Acts 22:6-10, as an example).

"Oh, happy day, that fixed my choice,
On Thee, my Savior and my God,
Well may this glowing heart rejoice,
And spread its raptures all abroad.
Happy day, happy day,
When Jesus washed my sins away;
He taught me how to watch and pray,
And live rejoicing every day,
Happy day, happy day,

When Jesus washed my sins away."

Let the three earliest converts in Philippi tell about their "first day." Lydia might say, "Yes, I remember that day very well . . ." Then she tells of the day when, in a quiet riverside prayer meeting, "the Lord opened her heart, and she gave attention to the things which Paul said" (Acts 16:13-14).Then the slave girl would give her testimony. She would tell of "that very moment" (Acts 16:18) when the evil spirit that had dominated her was driven out of her in the Name of Jesus (Acts 16:16-18).Then the jailer would say, "Do I remember it? How could I possible forget it? Without being irreverent, I could say that I met a Midnight Caller on the night of the 'jailhouse rock!'" What a first day! But now, it's your turn. You tell us about your first day. One man, describing his wedding day, said, "It seems just like yesterday — and you know what a lousy day yesterday was!" Well, your "first day" in Christ may have been full of heavy conviction and contrition, full of remorse and repentance, but the birds surely began to sing after the storm was over! The sun (Son) shined brightly when the thunderclouds were gone. Have you had your "first day" yet? Look at the calendar and note this date. This very day can be your "first day." Life that lasts forever with God in Heaven can begin for you at this very moment. Just as you had a "first day" of physical life, you can have a first day of spiritual life.

Then, Paul reminded them of the steady discipline of the continuation of their life in Christ. That "first day" was only a beginning. It was manifestly a miracle production of God — involving a miracle of vision (Acts 16:8-12) and of conversion, but the miracles were not over on the "first day." The fellowship of believers would withstand many an assault by the enemy, would experience much suffering (see Philippians 1:29), would chronicle many victories in Christ, would grow stronger and stronger in the Christian life, and would participate in the advance of the Gospel "alongside" the Apostle Paul. This continuation had lasted from ten to twelve years at the time of the Philippian letter, and it had involved a steady discipline on the part of the disciples in Philippi.

It is necessary to note the doctrinal connection between verses five and six. In verse six, the emphasis is on God's work, and it has been called "the preservation of the saints." In verse five, the emphasis is on their faithfulness, and it is called "the perseverance of the saints." Any doctrine of salvation or the Christian life that ignores either of these emphases is incomplete and unbalanced. The two sides of the Gospel are closely linked in these verses. The doctrine of Divine preservation (reflected in verse 6) declares that when God has begun the "good work" of transforming and qualifying grace in a believer, He will not leave it unfinished. He will perfect that work — and perfect us in the process!

> *"The work You have in me begun*
> *Shall by Your grace be fully done."*

The same Jesus Who said from the Cross, "It is finished," and "I have finished the work You gave Me to do," will one day say of us, "Here they are, Father, complete. I have finished the work in them You gave Me to do."

Here is a beautiful illustration of this truth from a book by Charles Wagner entitled *Happiness Is...* "In my house I have an easel which holds a picture of a mountain scene, typical of what you might see in the Pacific Northwest where I used to live. Included in the picture are a house and a stream. The painting isn't on my wall; it isn't even framed yet. You see, I'm not finished with it. One of these days I'm going to put the finishing touches on my work of art. You may or may not appreciate my painting when I'm through, but I wouldn't want you to pass judgment until I put the finishing touches on it. Believers are somewhat like that painting. They are God's 'work of art' (Eph. 2:10). The Lord is the Master Artist. He has chosen and arranged certain colors on the canvas of our lives already, some that we may not understand right now. But He knows what He is doing. He is working in our lives to complete the work of conforming us to the image of His dear Son."

Not only does Philippians 1:6 say something about how we should feel about what is happening in our lives, it should also have a bearing on the way we see others. Many people fall short of what we think they should be. It is somewhat easy, then, to pass judgment on them or to get impatient with them and their ways. But be patient. Don't spend too much time criticizing the little part of the painting you can see from a distance over the Artist's shoulder. The Lord Who has begun a good work in every believer will perfect it in His own time.

However, just as Paul emphasized the preservation of the saints in verse six, he also emphasized the perseverance of the saints in verse five. No saint of God will persevere without the mighty work of God's preservation, and conversely, God only preserves them by producing in them a might perseverance. Remember, it is "the security of the (continuing) believer," not the security of a practical unbeliever! The saints in Philippi had faithfully participated in the advance of the Gospel "from the first day until now," demonstrating by their perseverance God's great preservation. How admirable perseverance is among Christians!

Johann Sebastian Bach was perhaps the greatest composer of history. Bach had two consuming loves in his life: God and music. As is true of many geniuses, Bach wasn't much appreciated in his day. When he died in 1750 he was buried in an unmarked grave in a Leipzig, Germany, churchyard. It took dedicated musicians forty-six years just to collect all the music he had written, and it filled sixty huge printed volumes when the task was completed. Bach began to compose when he was nine years of age. He lived with a tyrannical older brother, who denied him the use of his musical library. However, Bach would slip into the library after everyone else was asleep and copy music by moonlight. After he had completed copying by hand every note of instrumental music in the library, his brother found it and burned it! But Bach didn't give up, and as a result he left a musical legacy that will long endure.

One of the most memorable speeches ever delivered was Winston Churchill's speech at a graduation exercise of Eaton College. Sir Winston simply said, briefly but dramatically, "Never, never, never...give up!"

Alexander Whyte, the great Scots preacher, said, "The perseverance of the saints consists in nothing less than an endless succession of new beginnings." Years ago, I came across a devotional gem while studying the book of Genesis. Jacob is blessing his twelve sons in Genesis 49 when he says of Gad, "A troop shall overcome him, but he shall overcome at the last" (Gen. 49:19). The first part of that sentence echoes the stark realism of life. We cannot expect an endless pattern of unbroken success in the spiritual life. The Christian life is not like a steady line climbing upward; it is more like a spiral with a lot of circles, and sometimes the direction is away from the target. But God is moving His child toward conformity to the image of Christ, and even the "setbacks" prove to be advantages as the believer perseveres. "A troop shall overcome him." You may find troops of adversity, troops of insult, troops of misunderstanding, troops of evil circumstance, troops of doubt, troops of temptation, coming against you to oppose you toe to toe. But "God is faithful, Who will not allow you to be tested beyond your ability, but will with the test provide a way of escape — that you may be able to bear it." Notice the line, "A troop shall overcome him." Perhaps you have been defeated, and you know how the sting of failure hurts. Be sure that the Philippians and all other saints knew that hurt, too. "But he shall overcome at last." God will preserve His child, and he will persevere! The Philippians had the same spirit of stubborn endurance that God builds into each of His children. The "until now" of verse five included many a day of mundane plodding, some setbacks, some conspicuous victories, and a lot of new beginnings. The "first day" of verse five leads to the final day of verse six.

> *"When life is pressing you down a bit*
> *Do what you must, but don't you quit!"*

Someone quipped that "a great oak is just a little nut that held its ground." William Carey was a giant of God who occupied a piece of ground for Christ's sake and then fought off all the "troops" that came against him. When the call came from God for him to go to India, every obstacle was put in his way. A lesser man would never have gone at all. When he finally did arrive in that desperate land, a troop overwhelmed him. Death took one of his children. His wife went insane. For years he worked without one native convert. But Carey simply would not give up. One day, someone mentioned the possibility of writing his life story. Carey said, "Should that happen, if the writer mentions that I am a plodder, he will describe me justly. Anything beyond this will be too much. I can plod. I can persevere in any definite pursuit which I believe to be of God. To this, I owe everything."

The Philippians did not have a "flash in the pan" Christianity. They didn't "go up like a rocket, and come down like a rock." Their faith was not like a flash fire which quickly reduces to a pile of ashes. When they "signed on," they signed on "for the duration." I once heard an African-American pastor preach on the first words of Acts 2:42, "And they continued steadfastly," and he added four words of his own: "They continued steadfastly — and they didn't stop!" It was a remarkable and memorable message on perseverance in faith and service. The Philippians set a precedent for such a message. They had a remarkable history of steadiness and endurance. "Let us run with endurance the race that is set before us" (Hebrews 12:1). The entire Philippian fellowship was a pattern of perseverance.

Finally, Paul reminds them of the coming climax, the consummation, the "grand finale" of the Christian life. He mentions the coming "day of Christ Jesus." On that day, all of God's work in the believer and in the fellowship of saints will reach its crown. On that day, Jesus will be manifested in glory, will be met by His glorified Bride, will judge our service for Him, and will praise us (I Cor. 4:5) and reward us for our faithfulness to Him. We look back to the "first day," and we look forward to the final day. While others keep their eye on the clock, we should keep our eye on the Coming! We stand today somewhere between the "from" and the "until" of verse five.

A dear, dear pastor friend of mine signs his letters, "Until the Unto." Perhaps we should sign ours, "Between the from and the until." Thank You, Jesus, for what You have already done! We eagerly look forward to the rest — in both senses of the word. Until then, keep us faithful in advancing the Gospel.

Chapter 3

Listening to the Prayer of a Disciple-Maker

And this I pray, that your love may abound still more and more in knowledge and in all discernment, That you may approve the things that are excellent, that you may be sincere and without offense till the day of Christ, Being filled with the fruits of righteousness which are by Jesus Christ, to the glory and praise of God (Philippians 1:9-11).

Be careful to note the order of the opening verses of Philippians one. Note that in verses three through seven, Paul praises the Philippians for their progress, and then in verses nine through eleven, he prays for their perfecting. Note that he praises first, and prays later. He points out the actual, then appeals for the possible. He rehearses the real, then requests the ideal.

Listen to a man's regular prayers and you can tell his heart. Prayer is the index of a man's soul, the barometer of his heart. Prayer is the thermometer that registers his spiritual temperature. Several of Paul's prayers are recorded, and they expose a cosmopolitan Christian with great and expansive relationships with other people. One need not wonder why God used Paul in such a mighty way; he can find out by feeling his "prayer pulse". It has been said that "God always uses the vessel that is closest at hand." Paul said, "The Lord is at hand" (as near as my hand), and God might have said,

"Paul is at hand." God always had ready access to Paul as His vehicle. This is clearly revealed in Paul's prayers.

Intercessory prayer is absolutely essential in a disciple-maker's life. The moment words are used prayerlessly and people are treated prayerlessly, something essential begins to leak out of life. In Tennyson's <u>Morte d' Arthur,</u> these lines are found: "More things are wrought by prayer than this world dreams of. Wherefore, let thy voice rise like a fountain for me night and day." Paul prayed as if he were perfectly aware of this rule and heard this request from his disciple daily. The greatest secret of Paul's disciple-making ministry is his prayer life, and one of the major keys of his prayer life is its focus on disciples and their needs.

No Christian can afford to ignore the lessons of Paul's prayer-life, or the lessons in each recorded prayer of the great Apostle. Indeed, to study the themes and subjects of Paul's recorded prayers is a vast education in eternal things. Let me show this by placing three of his prayers and their themes in a systematic succession of my choosing. In Ephesians 1:15-19, there is a *prayer for the enlightenment of believers*. In Philippians 1:9-11, our text, there is a *prayer for the enrichment of believers*. In Ephesians 3:14-21, there is a *prayer for the enlargement of believers*. If you combine these prayers and list their specific themes, you discover that the Apostle prays that his readers may overflow in spiritual wisdom, in full relational knowledge, in personal dynamic, in faithful endurance, in longsuffering, in joy, in gratitude, and in love. An in-depth study of Paul's eight recorded prayers might well be more valuable to a disciple-maker than a seminary degree! If you do not know how to pray for a disciple, master the prayers of Paul. They are inspired prayers, and you may always count on an answer from heaven when you pray these prayers for a disciple. One of the many disciple-making prayers of Paul is recorded in Philippians 1:9-11. Paul's supreme desire for the Philippians is the highest purpose of the Gospel of Christ for all of us. Let's explore this great prayer.

THE PRACTICAL DIMENSIONS OF A DISCIPLE-MAKER'S PRAYER

Here we can see the *practical dimensions* of all prayer, and especially of a disciple-maker's prayer. How *incredibly peculiar* prayer is! Note the word "prayer" in verse four, and the word "pray" in verse nine, and stop to analyze the exercise of prayer for just a moment. How strange it is! Prayer is a bit like a one-way phone call to someone you've never seen, heard, or touched — and there is not even an audible voice at the other end! Prayer is totally an exercise of faith, based on the bare revelation of the Word of God.

When you go through the "drive-through" lane at a MacDonald's restaurant, the first thing you do is to speak into a box. Into a box, mind you! You don't see a face, though you do hear a voice. But when a sack containing the food you ordered is thrust out of a nearby window, you know your "supplication" has been heard! Prayer is like that: you pray "sight unseen", but then, behold, the "sack containing your order" appears, and you know God has heard and answered your prayer. Intercessory prayer majors on the invisible. The people Paul prayed for in this prayer were far away and invisible, but prayer could reach them! He was praying to God, who was also invisible, but prayer could reach Him! The thing he prayed for, "your love," is an invisible commodity, but prayer could influence it! The qualities he prayed for, "knowledge and discernment," are invisible commodities, but prayer can determine them! The "excellence" and "the fruits of righteousness" which he prayed for are immeasurable and invisible, but God can produce and instill them in answer to prayer. Prayer, though mighty, is an incredibly peculiar exercise.

Prayer is an *intensely personal exercise.* "I pray," Paul said. Remember the life of Paul. Before he became a Christian, he was a "Pharisee of the Pharisees." Jesus told us about the prayer life of a Pharisee. "The Pharisee struck a pose and prayed thus with himself." The Pharisees called attention to themselves when they prayed. But when Paul was converted, the Lord sent Ananias to him, saying, "Behold, he prayeth." It is as if he actually prayed for the very first time. When we think we pray, does heaven think we are praying? Does heaven say, "Behold, he is praying"?

Note the words, "every prayer of mine" in verse four, and the words "I pray" in verse nine. In verse three, Paul said, "I thank my God." Churches may influence God through united prayer, and corporate prayer movements are often powerful in moving the Hand that moves the world, but prayer is essentially a personal thing. "The effectual, fervent prayer of a righteous man availeth much." No one prays by proxy, in spite of the heresy that certain individuals store up merit for the use of others. Each believer approaches God personally through Jesus Christ, and engages personally in the great exercise of prayer in the Throne Chamber of the universe.

True prayer is to be an *interminably persistent exercise*. In the Greek language, the word translated "pray" in verse nine is a present tense verb. The Greek present tense emphasizes continuous action. Paul's statement then could be translated like this: "This I keep on praying." He didn't just pray a few times for the Philippians and then forget about them; he made it a habit to pray for them. Jesus said, "Men ought always to pray, and not to give up." Paul said that we are to "pray without ceasing," and this rule has a special application to a disciple-maker.

A disciple-maker's prayer should be an *intentionally purposeful* prayer. "And this I pray, that..." This is a purpose clause, showing both the reason and the content of Paul's prayer. I only mention this here, because we will explore the content of his prayer later in this study. Someone has wisely said, "If you aim at nothing, you will hit it every time." Prayer in general accomplishes nothing in particular. Question: If God answered a prayer for you today, would you know He had answered it? Here, Paul's prayer draws dead aim on some indispensable realities in a believer's life.

Finally, a disciple-maker's prayers are *immeasurable powerful*. One person can shake the world through prayer. One person's prayers can have more power than all the influential people of a community combined. God promises great blessings and great power in answer to prayer. But we must not allow ourselves to be deceived at this point. What kind of power does God give in answer to prayer? What is the primary outcome of true prayer? Not "Boom" power, but "Blessing" power. Many Christians immediately think of "Boom" power when they hear that the Greek word for power is "dunamis", the word from which we get our word, "dynamite." However, the Greeks did not have dynamite (which wasn't invented until Alfred Nobel), and thus they had no concept of that kind of power when they heard the word "dunamis." The better word is "dynamic". Someone defined power as "the forceful expression of personality," and this certainly provides a good definition of God's power. God's primary attributes are holiness and love, and we may expect God's power to produce these attributes in us. So prayer produces character and conduct power, the power of illumination, sanctification, communication, conviction, transformation, etc.

These, then, are the practical dimensions of a disciple-maker's prayer. It is incredibly peculiar, intensely personal, interminably persistent, intentionally purposeful, and will prove to be immeasurably powerful. Now let's press on into the content of the prayer.

THE PARTICULAR DESIRES OF A DISCIPLE-MAKER'S PRAYER

In verses nine through eleven, Paul specifies the *particular desires* he has in his heart for his disciples in Philippi.

Paul desires the *relational graciousness* of his disciples. I am praying for "your love," he tells them. He prays for the enlargement of their love — "that your love may abound still more and more." He prays for the enlightenment of their love — "in knowledge and in all discernment." He prays for the enrichment of their love — "that you may be sincere and without offense." He prays for the employment of their love — "that you may approve things that are excellent." He prays for the endurance of their love — "till the day of Christ." And he prays for the expression of their love — "being filled with the fruits of righteousness which are by Jesus Christ." You see, the love of Christ is like a vast ocean, and so should be the love of His disciples!

Paul desires the *regular growth* of his disciples. "That your love may abound still more and more." Paul had earlier expressed this same desire for the Thessalonian believers when he wrote, "And the Lord make you to increase and abound in love one toward another, and toward all men, even as we do toward you" (I Thess. 3:12). The Philippians had already experienced the inflow of Christ's love at conversion, but Paul is praying here that the lake of their love may rise higher and higher, overflowing its previous perimeters "still more and more." The picture conjured by the word "abound" is that of a bucket standing under a giant waterfall, with the water flowing over all sides because the bucket cannot possibly contain the downpour. Christians sing a song which includes these words, "I've got love like a river." When a person is saved love inflows his heart. "The love of God is shed abroad in our hearts by the Holy Spirit who is given unto us" (Romans 5:5). And the inflow of love will lead to the overflow and outflow of love. Every Christian should seek to overflow his present capacity to love, his present concept of love, and his present communication of love. And since Paul was praying for this abundance of love, we know that such love must come for God, not from within ourselves.

Paul also desires the *real genuineness* of his disciples. "This I pray, that your love may abound still more and more in knowledge and in all discernment; that ye may approve things that are excellent; that ye may be sincere and without offence till the day of Christ." Though a believer's love may be like a river in flood-time, its volume needs to be brought within certain guiding limitations. Its flow must be restrained by the two river banks of "knowledge and judgment." A river without restraining banks becomes a stagnant swamp. Love is not just an ocean of emotion, as many people think it is. True love is solidly based on wise spiritual perception. Genuine Christian love is produced and controlled by the Holy Spirit through the truth (that is, through the Word of God). Thus its fullest exercise can only spring from a knowledge of the truth. The world may say that "love is blind," but nothing could be further from the truth. True love is bound by accurate perception, and that perception sharpens the exercise of love. In other words, love should be discerning and discriminating. The word "discernment" (or judgment, KJV) is *aisthesis*, and it describes the ability of the inner man to separate not only the good from the bad, but also the important from the unimportant, and in each case choosing the best and rejecting the other possibilities.

Many believers seem to possess a dynamic love, but they lack the restraints of "knowledge and all discernment." Paul was not impressed by those who had love or zeal without knowledge. Concerning his fellow Israelites, he wrote, "I bear them record that they have a zeal for God, but not according to knowledge" (Rom. 10:2). The learning of many is not balanced by love, and the love of many is not balanced by learning. There is a kind of Christian who will demonstrate great eagerness and enthusiasm, and his motives and intentions cannot be faulted, but he often does far more harm than good. And he is often extremely vulnerable to doctrinal error and the misleading of questionable leaders. How does he get this knowledge and discernment? By hanging around Jesus Christ and all the people and exercises that truly reflect Him! This requires a long process of relationship and growth, and cannot be gained in an "express lane." So the novice Christian must not protrude himself into positions and practices that should belong only to the maturing and discerning believer.

A little girl found her little pet kitten out in the rain one day, soaking wet. Because she loved the shivering animal, she took it into the house and turned on the oven in the kitchen. She then tenderly placed the cat in the oven to warm it up and dry it out. You can well imagine the devastating result! The cat came out looking like a piece of toasted leather! Her love was well-intentioned, but not well-informed. She lacked the restraints of "knowledge and all discernment." A father or mother may ruin a child by overindulgence; unwise love may do far more harm than good. A wife killed her husband and then flung herself across his dead body, exclaiming, "I loved him; I loved him so much." Personally, I would rather be loved a little less (and more wisely) and live longer! "That ye may approve things that are excellent." This phrase refers to the actual choice of the best over anything less than the best. The preceding phrase refers to the discrimination of the two, and this phrase refers to the decision for the best over the less-than-best. Excellence only has one dimension, and that is height. It calls us to the summits of life. It is not content when we merely escape the pit; it is not satisfied when we only leave the swamp lands of low living. It is not even content when we top the foothills and look back upon the dismal depths from which we have been lifted. It keeps saying, "Come up higher! Come up higher!" And our hearts echo, "Lord, plant my feet on higher ground." The word "excellent" should be held as an ideal for every area of our lives — to such things as our reading, our recreation, our relationships, our routines, etc. To "approve things that are excellent" will mean that we test all things and discriminate morally and spiritually between them. I well remember the little poem I was taught in childhood, "Good, better, best, never let it rest, until the good is better, and the better is best." How I wish I had always applied that rule!

> *"God has His best things for the few*
> *Who dare to stand the test;*
> *God has His second choice for those*
> *Who will not have His best."*

"That ye may be sincere and without offense until the day of Christ." The word "sincere" contains a combination of ideas in it, "tested by sunlight," and "without wax." The background of the word is very picturesque. In Paul's day, skilled craftsmen made beautiful porcelain pottery. Sometimes it would crack when fired. They might fill the cracks with wax and sell them as perfect pieces. But when placed in the sunlight or in a heated room, the wax would melt and the flaw would be exposed. The Latin term, "sine cera," from which we derive our word, "sincere," means, "without wax." An honest dealer would advertise his product as being "without wax." So Paul's prayer may be paraphrased, "I pray that you will be completely transparent." I pray that you will not doctor yourself to look one way when you are actually another. That you will be without hypocrisy. A Christian must make it his life's vocation to be pure, genuine, honest, free from sham and pretense.

Then note the term, "without offense." The word "sincere" probably refers to one's relationship with God, while this term concerns one's relationship with his fellow men. The word "sincere" basically means "unmixed, unalloyed." The term "without offense" means "without stumbling block." "Offense" is the word *skandalon*, from which we get our word "scandal." It is elsewhere translated "stumbling-block." Every believer is at every moment either a "stepping stone" or a "stumbling block" in the lives of others. So the Christian must strive to keep out of his life anything that might cause anyone else to stumble morally or spiritually. The old Scottish preacher, John Henry Jowett, said he was visiting in a British town when he saw a strange sight. He saw a sigh painted on a street lamp advertising the public baths of the town. But the street lamp was absolutely filthy! Jowett said it is equally inconsistent, and far more hypocritical, for Christians to point toward the Calvary bath, toward Jesus' blood, toward cleanliness in Him, when they are covered with sin and filth.

And Paul indicates that our obligation extends to the very "day of Christ." In a factory or a school or an office, workers often live with their eyes on the clock. Christians should live with their eyes, not on the clock, but on the Coming! What an incredible prayer for the real genuineness of the disciple!

Then Paul prays for the *rare greatness* of his disciples. He prays that they may "be filled with the fruits of righteousness, which are by Jesus Christ." The preceding phrases are negative, but this phrase presents the positive side. Again, Paul prays his disciples toward the highest heights. The tree that bears fruit is alive, but the tree that is filled with fruit has abundant life. "He that abideth in me, and I in Him," said Jesus, "the same bringeth forth much fruit. Herein is My Father glorified, that ye bear much fruit." This is the "fruit of righteousness," or "the fruit that proceeds from righteousness." Notice that it is not fruit which you produce; it is "by Jesus Christ." Thus, it is dependent upon the personal power of Jesus Christ Himself, and upon a continual abiding in Him before the fruit can be borne. Which end of the branch is our concern, the fruit-bearing end, or the connecting end? Obviously, the connecting point should command our total interest. If you have any more worries than the small, round area of the branch where it connects with the trunk, you have too many. And if you don't have that one, you don't have enough.

This prayer has no spiritual boundaries. It is cosmopolitan and limitless. What a difference it would make if all believers earnestly entreated our Father with this prayer in behalf of other Christians. What a difference it would make if all disciple-makers prayed this prayer for their disciples, and all disciples for their disciple-makers, and all disciples for each other.

THE PERMANENT DESIGNS OF A DISCIPLE-MAKER'S PRAYER

The stated motive of Paul's prayer, the intended outcome of it, is the same motive and the same intended outcome for all things Christian — "to the glory and praise of God." *Here are the permanent designs of all prayer.*

Every true Christian desires that God may receive *proper attention*, and this is the *permanent design* of the disciple-maker's prayer. "To the glory of God." The word "glory" in the Old Testament means "weight" or "heaviness." We reflect this today when we hear a vast truth and we say, "That's heavy!" God is heavy, weighty, and will be a burden -- either in the happiest or most horrible sense of that word. Anybody carries certain "burdens" because of any relationship that he did not have without that relationship. Then the word "glory" also carries the idea of radiance or splendor. So the word "glory" refers to the display of God's character. We all have sinned and fallen short of the "glory of God" (Rom. 3:23). This means that each of us is less perfect than God is.

But once saved, we are to "do all things to the glory of God." So our lives are truly to be God's Temple (I Cor. 6:19, 3:16), and a temple is simply a shrine where a God is exhibited. Glory has to do with the demonstration, the exhibition, the outshining of God's character, and this exhibition is to take place through each Christian. The desire for God's glory is that He will be seen by men as He really is. The highest glory of God on earth comes from the gradual increase in the disciple's likeness to Christ. Christians have been called "the secretaries of God's praise." That great honor and responsibility lies on each believer. If your community depended totally on you for its only visible display of God, how much of Him would it see?

Finally, every true Christian desires that God may receive *proper adoration,* and this is the permanent design of the disciple-maker's prayer. "And to the praise of God." Your salvation began with God in eternity (Phil. 1:6), and that which began at the Throne of God in Heaven must finally return to its point of origin. That which began with the love and grace of God must recycle back to God "to His glory and praise." "For of Him, and through Him, and to Him are all things" (Rom. 11:36)." Praise and prayer go together. Praise is like the follow-through in a golf swing. An amateur golfer usually loses great power in his golf swing because he does not know the vast importance of a proper follow-through in the swing. Praise without prayer is presumption, but prayer without praise is ingratitude. Augustine said, "A Christian should be a hallelujah from head to foot." I pray for a passion to obey Jesus in making disciples, and for understanding and fervor in praying this prayer for them — "TO THE GLORY AND PRAISE OF GOD."

Chapter 4

God's Surprise Party for the Disciple-Maker

Now I want you to know and continue to rest assured, brethren, that what (has happened) to me (this imprisonment,) has actually only served to advance and give a renewed impetus to the (spreading of the) good news — of the Gospel. So much is this a fact that throughout the whole imperial guard and to all the rest (here), my imprisonment has become generally known to be in Christ — in that I am a prisoner in His service and for Him. And (also) most of the brethren have derived fresh confidence in the Lord because of my chains, and are much more bold to speak and publish fearlessly the Word of God — acting with more freedom and indifference to the consequences (Philippians 1:12-14, Amplified Bible)

Underscore the word "actually" in the above text, and read it with heavy emphasis on that word. The King James translation says that "the things which happened unto me have fallen out rather unto the furtherance of the Gospel." The word translated "actually" in the Amplified Bible and "rather" in the King James Version indicates that the outcome specified in the text was quite different than Paul and others anticipated in the circumstances of Paul's life.

Everybody is familiar with the phrase, "a blessing in disguise." There are many things in life that, at first glance, seem undesirable but turn out to be very advantageous, extremely beneficial, in short — a blessing. Some things which are very unpleasant at the moment of their occurrence turn out to be great blessings as we view them in retrospect.

Any believer in Christ who has sought to walk with Him for a long time knows that life in Christ is free and replete with creative possibilities — both human and divine. The God who created this universe is surely not short of creative ideas! And the world that He made was not only created, but it remains very creative. And this is especially true for God's Spirit-walking child. Many remarkable and amazing things take place when we live by faith. When we believe that God has created us in His image, when we trust that He loves us and works out His salvation in us (Philippians 2:13), when we decide that the only way in which life takes on meaning is when we believe that the invisible truth is what keeps the visible world together, certain things begin to happen in our lives apart from our efforts. They surprise us with their presence. Or rather, God surprises us by their intrusion into our lives. The God who created us and re-created us in Christ Jesus, continues to work creatively in us and for us and through us. He keeps bringing new qualities and new realities into our lives, and He continues adding surprising lines to our "script." There is a "larger script," a large picture, and we play from that script, we color within those lines — but then we are almost free to "ad lib" inside of the Big Picture all the way home! And the Holy Spirit is always changing our lines and repainting our picture in incredibly creative ways.

I "stumbled onto" a surprising paragraph about surprises in a book by Sue Monk Kidd entitled, <u>God's Joyful Surprises (!)</u>. Let me record it in entirety. "When I was small and my father arrived home from work, I would race to the door to greet him. Now and then I would find him standing there with his hands behind his back. 'Pick a hand,' he would say. These words touched me like an electric current. For I knew, hidden behind my father, buried in the fold of one of his hands, there was a surprise meant for me. 'This one!' I would shout, pointing wildly. And he would whisk out his hand and slowly, too slowly, uncurl his fingers. And finally there it would be, shining in his palm, a gift I could not have imagined. A golden paper ring from one of my granddaddy's cigars to wear on my finger, a cardinal feather for my hair or sometimes a silver nickel. I have not thought of it until now, but it seems my father's surprises had a curious way of coming on the days I needed them most. The days I fell off my bicycle or went to the doctor with a sore throat or broke something irreplaceable in the house. I suppose Mother told him. Somehow he knew that I needed to be surprised with a gift of love that would help bind up my broken day.

Now I like to think of myself as grown up. Yet I cannot seem to get rid of the longing to search my father's hand. Perhaps that's why I have found such joy in discovering that God is a God of infinite surprises."

It's a long way from the idyllic world of a child which is full of only tiny happinesses and heartbreaks to the pressurized, poignant, power-packed world of the Apostle Paul. God's surprises continue, but they are much more surprising, unique, and peculiar than those in a child's life. The surprises are not always "happy" in the weak and sentimental sense of that word, but they are far more amazing and gratifying from the viewpoint of eternity.

The Apostle Paul was a great missionary and maker of disciples. One would be hard-pressed to try to prove which of these two profiles was the more important in his life. These two activities were well-balanced in his life. Today, many Christians are like a lop-sided bicycle tire that causes the bike to go flopping down the street. Some "bulge" on the side of missions, others on the side of preaching, others on the side of disciple-making. No Christian leader would find it easy to plead guilty to the charge of imbalance, but the sad facts shout their testimony to us. "The actual figures are that the Christian world receives 99 percent of all Christian literature, 90.9 percent of all foreign missionaries, 95 percent of all full-time Christian workers and 99.9 percent of all output from Christian radio/TV. Even overseas 'mission field' churches are clamoring for mission funds for their own local needs while mission vision for the fields still beyond receives only about 10 percent of mission monies and personnel" (<u>Penetrating Missions' Final Frontier,</u> by Ted Yamamori). The Apostle Paul can show us the way to attain balance between home and foreign ministries, and between missions, evangelism and disciple-making.

Paul was a great strategist. He knew the value of cities in Gospel pioneering. He knew that cities were the headwaters of the world, and that if a Gospel seed were dropped into those headwaters, the current might carry it anywhere. Paul had ministered in Jerusalem, the heart of Palestine and Judaism; at Antioch, the heart of Syria; at Ephesus, the heart of Asia Minor; and at Athens, the heart of Greece. There was one more cosmopolitan city that he longed to visit, the city of Rome. Take a few minutes and read and meditate on Romans 1:8-13, and see the heart of the missionary-strategist leap from the page. It was obviously Paul's desire — and plan — to go to Rome. He surely thought he would get there "as usual," paying his own fare, moving freely as he wished through the city, and being welcomed by the saints of the small church there. But surprise, surprise! He wanted to go there as a preacher, but instead, he went as a prisoner. And out of this circumstance ("circum" — around; "stance" — to stand; circumstance is that which surrounds us) came one of the great "eureka experiences" of the Bible. A serendipity of the first heavenly magnitude was in store for this great missionary and disciple-maker.

GOD'S GOSPEL SEQUENCES

There are certain steps that are taken when God's Gospel strategy is followed. These are specified in Romans 10:13-15, which says, "Whosoever shall call upon the name of the Lord shall be saved. How then shall they call on him in whom they have not believed? And how shall they believe in him of whom they have not heard? And how shall they hear without a preacher? And how shall they preach, except they be sent?" God wants His Word to the lived, but before it can be lived, it must be believed. Before it can be believed, however, it must be heard. But before it can be heard, it must be preached. Before it can be preached, the preacher must be called and sent. The miracle-marked work of God at Philippi had followed this order. God had sent the missionary team of Paul and Silas, even working dramatically to close doors in other directions and giving a special vision to them to direct them to Philippi (Acts 16:6-10). Two of God's great surprises took place at Troas, one being the guiding vision about southern Europe, the other being the enlistment and addition of Dr. Luke to Paul's missionary team.

"Faith comes by hearing, and hearing by the Word of God," says Romans 10:17. After the missionary team was sent to Philippi, they had preached the Gospel there. The circumstance of each Gospel presentation was different, but the same Gospel was preached. It was heard by a wealthy business woman named Lydia, by a poor slave girl, and by the jailer of a Roman jail in the colony of Philippi. In each case, a miracle of salvation and deliverance occurred. Each believed and was saved. This Gospel sequence is normal and typical. There is nothing surprising in the sequence that was followed. The surprises developed in succeeding years as God's plan carried Paul to Rome. The letter to the Philippians was written from Rome — where Paul was in prison. Now for the rest of the story . . .

GOD'S GRACIOUS SOVEREIGNTY

The people of Philippi have watched anxiously as God's plan to evangelize Rome has unfolded. Of all the churches of Paul's travels, they have been most involved in his financial support and in prayer and personal interest. They undoubtedly had prayed for Paul to get to Rome, as he had so earnestly hoped. But neither of them expected his trip to Rome to follow such a pattern. We may establish these rules: The steps of a good man are ordered of the Lord; the stops of a good man are orchestrated of the Lord; the stumblings of a good man are overcome of the Lord; and the schedule of a good man is overseen and overruled by the Lord. Our text provides a great example of rule numbers one, two, and four in that list. Paul's steps, stops, and schedule were in the sovereign hand of God. Robert Louis Stevenson, whose body was wracked with pain and disease, nonetheless testified, "I came about like a well-handled ship. There stood at the wheel that little-known steersman named God."

"Disappointment is His appointment, Change one letter, then I see
That the thwarting of my purpose Is God's better choice for me.
His appointment must be blessing, Tho' it may come in disguise,
For the end from the beginning Open to His wisdom lies.
Disappointment is His appointment, No good will He withhold,
From denials oft we gather Treasures of His love untold.
Well He knows each broken purpose Leads to fuller, deeper trust,
And the end of all His dealings Proves our God is wise and just.
Disappointment is His appointment, Lord, I take it, then, as such,
Like clay in the hands of a potter, Yielding wholly to Thy touch.
My life's plan is Thy molding, Not one single choice is mine;
Let me answer, unrepining — 'Father, not my will, but Thine.'"

Albert Einstein said, "I shall never believe that God plays dice with the world," and I agree with him. Paul was not a pawn in enemy hands, and neither are we. We have been carefully selected by a loving Father, and it is His desire to deploy us in the world for both His best advantage and ours. That advantage is often gained in peculiar ways, but when the final scheme is seen, we will recognize perfectly that "our God does all things well." As C. S. Lewis said, "A secret Master of Ceremonies has been at work. But we must remember that God is nobody but Himself and what He does is like nothing else." One pastor took several months and did nothing but read the Book of Revelation to his church in the Sunday evening services. The reading was entirely without explanation or comment. He later said, "I've never seen or experienced anything so powerful in all my life. I was reminded again by the Word of God that anything can be endured if we know the outcome is certain." Paul Borthwick, in his book on missions, noted that it was the tsetse fly of Africa, which carries sleeping sickness, that stopped Islam's advance (by the effects the fly had on the Muslims and their camels) into Africa, and allowed the great movement of the Holy Spirit which is continuing there until this day.

*"Careless seems the great Avenger, History's pages but record
One death-grapple, in the darkness, `Twixt old systems and the
Word.
Truth forever on the scaffold, Wrong forever on the throne,
Yet that scaffold sways the future, And, behind the dim unknown,
Standeth God within the shadows, Keeping watch upon His own."*

GOD'S GREAT SURPRISES

"My circumstances have produced instead the advance of the Gospel." Instead of what? Instead of the feared and expected outcome. Both Paul and the Philippians had thought that his ministry might be over when he was taken to Rome in chains. But again, the circumstances were controlled — even planned — by God. Think for a moment of the past experiences Paul alluded to when he wrote of "my circumstances." These circumstances are recorded partially in Acts 21-28. During the three years before he wrote the Philippian letter, he had experienced imprisonment (again!), harassment (again!), and threats against his life (again!). But Paul's attention was not on himself, and so he bypassed the graphic details and, instead, emphasized that God had rigged a great surprise so that the Gospel was advanced, and not hindered, by his circumstances.

The word "furtherance" or "pioneer advance" is a fabulous word in explaining the outcome of his "prison ministry" in Rome. The Gospel had originally come to Philippi as a pioneer advance, and now it was advancing in Rome the same way. Paul no doubt recalled the time in the Philippian jail when he and Silas had been praying on the inside of the jail and Timothy and the new Christians in Lydia's house had been praying on the outside. God had said a loud "Amen" to their prayers by sending an earthquake. The Roman jailer was saved and then his entire household, adding substantially to the tiny infant church in Philippi. Now God was at it again! Paul was in prison again, and again his jailers were being saved!

Think of the contributions of Christians in captivity. Daniel Defoe wrote <u>Robinson Crusoe</u> while in prison. John Bunyan wrote <u>Pilgrim's Progress</u> during his twelve-year stay in Bedford jail. Sir

Walter Raleigh wrote his great work, <u>The History of the World,</u> during thirteen years in jail. Martin Luther translated the Bible and fanned the flames of the Reformation while imprisoned in the castle at Wartburg. Dante wrote brilliantly during his twenty years in prison, part of the time spent under a death sentence. Adoniram Judson, the famous missionary to Burma, spent a great portion of his first fourteen years in confinement and terrible tortures in a Burmese jail. He himself declared that he prayed that "he might live to translate the entire Bible into the native language, and to preside over a native church of at least one hundred members" -- and God answered both of those prayers. This rehearsal of the sufferings of saints reminds us of two lessons:

First, Christians should know that "fiery trials" are a real part of their contract as Christians.

Second, Christians should know that the Lord always has a better idea. Remember that, in spite of momentary appearance, "God is able to do exceeding abundantly above all that we ask or even think of asking, according to the power that works in us" (remember that this, too, was written from that same Roman prison). "God makes all things work together for good to those who love Him and are the called according to His purpose."

The word "furtherance" is a great word with a great history. The word was used in the first century to refer to a corps of engineers or a company of woodcutters preceding the travel of a dignitary or the progress of an army, cutting a road through a forest so that unimpeded progress could be made. Paul is declaring that his circumstances are like Divine wood cutters, cutting a way through the opposition so that the Gospel might be advanced. So we can deduce this principle for today's disciple-maker: The things that seem to hedge us in, the things that apparently hinder and handicap us, may be used of God as Divinely appointed woodcutters to hew out a path for the greater advance of the Gospel.

Let's see this principle at work in Paul's case, and then we will show some illustrations and applications for today. Paul's liberty was gone. He could not even go to church or to the marketplace, let alone to a pulpit. Or so it seemed! Again, God had a whole set of surprises behind His back. Look at the outcome.

First, there were *new converts* to the Gospel among the Roman soldiers. In verse 13, Paul says that "throughout the whole imperial guard, my imprisonment has become generally known to be in Christ." And in Philippians 4:22, Paul referred to "all the saints in Ceasar's household." What a stroke for the Gospel! The word used is "praetorium," the word for the elite imperial guard of 10,000 select soldiers assigned to protect the Roman Emperor and guard all imperial prisoners (Paul was one of them). Just think of it. Paul was under constant guard (Acts 28:16, 20). The guards remained for six hours at a time. So at least four a day provided him a "captive audience!" And each one was a potential convert and Gospel messenger! The fact that Paul was Christ's prisoner "became manifest throughout the Roman guard." In other words, the fact that he was there as a Christian became the talk of the town. I can imagine the drift of their conversations. The question of the reason for Paul's imprisonment would inevitably be raised, and the word was passed around that it was because of his relationship to Christ. The next question would be, "Who is Christ?" And we can be certain that Paul supplied the fuel for a full Gospel apologetic. What an opportunity, and all funded by the Roman government!

Two Jewish bounty hunters found themselves surrounded by 10,000 Arabs. The young novice said despairingly, "What are we going to do?" The veteran replied gleefully, "Do? We're going to get rich, that's what we're going to do!" Paul must have thought, "They've got me surrounded; they can't all get away!" Never before had Paul had such an audience, and they were chained to him — a truly "captive audience!" I guess you could call the result a "chain reaction!" Acts 28:30, 31 says, "He stayed two full years in his own rented quarters, and was welcoming all who came to him, preaching the kingdom of God, and teaching concerning the Lord Jesus with all openness, unhindered" (NASV). Paul was not behind bars; he was under "house arrest." His case was important enough that he was bound to a guard day and night. Can you imagine the kind of truths that flowed from the mouth of the man who wrote such letters as Romans, Galatians, and I Corinthians! And you may be sure that those Roman soldiers heard his words with intensifying interest, and investigated his life as with a fine-tooth comb. They saw his life, they heard his testimony, they observed his companions, they audited his teaching, they overheard his prayers, and they listened as he dictated his correspondence! And there were new soldiers of Christ enlisted from the Emperor's elite guard. What a surprise!

Second, there was a *new communication* of the Gospel throughout the city and the surrounding area. Hear Paul's words: "My bonds in Christ are manifest...in all other places." The word for the communication of the Gospel that is used in verse 14 is not the word for formal presentation, like preaching or systematic teaching, but rather it is the word for "everyday conversation." The Gospel was gossiped everywhere! Not just Paul, but Jesus, became the talk of the town! What a surprise!

Third, there was *new courage* among the Christians of Rome. It took quite a lot of courage to preach Jesus Christ in pagan Rome, and it seems that many true believers had become "closet Christians" or "secret saints" rather than risking their lives for what they believed. But many of them became "turned on" by Paul's courageous witness. If Paul could take so much abuse for the Gospel's sake, they could certainly take a little heat too! So verse 14 says that "the saints at Rome were much more bold to speak the Word without fear." Paul's faithful witness stimulated a volume of testimony about Jesus from their lives. In the medical world, where transplants have become incredibly common, operations have been performed by which one man's nerve has been implanted into another man's body. But God has been doing this for a long time. The nerve of the Apostle Paul had given nerve to other saints to speak more boldly. Remember, Christian, it was when the Jerusalem authorities "saw the boldness of Peter and John, that they took knowledge of them that they had been with Jesus." To be intimidated among men is to be incriminated before God. Be bold!

Paul wrote, "Watch ye, stand fast in the faith, quit you like men, be strong" (I Cor. 16:13), and here, he was the very personification of his own exhortation. And many others were emboldened by his example. What a surprise!

Fourth, there is one last great bonus surprise that came out of Paul's imprisonment and sufferings. There was a *new correspondence* for the church in all ages. Do you realize how much blessing came out of apparently evil circumstances in Paul's life — with Rome at the center? He had wanted to go to Rome earlier, and God hindered him. What was the outcome? The book of Romans. Surprise, surprise. We have the Book of Romans because God seemed to coldly disregard Paul's long-standing ambition to preach the Gospel in Rome. Then, finally, God let Paul go to Rome — as a prisoner. And what was the outcome? He wrote the books of Ephesians, Philippians, Colossians, and Philemon while in prison in Rome. It was God's surprising prohibition that led to the writing of the Book of Romans, and it was God's surprising permission that led to the writing of the Books of Ephesians, Philippians, Colossians, and Philemon. What incredible surprises! The Greek word for Paul's chain is *halusis*. Should we not say, "Hallelujah for the *halusis!*"

Paul must have felt a little like Martin Niemoller, who wrote many years later from a Nazi prison camp, "I believe my imprisonment is a singular instance of God's holy sense of humor. Here they laugh scornfully, 'at last we've got him,' and arrest eight hundred more, but what is the result? Full churches with praying congregations. It would be utter ingratitude to become bitter in the face of such facts." Or like the great French author, Victor Hugo (my all-time favorite novel is his monumental work, *Les Miserables*), who was exiled by Napoleon III for nineteen years. His biographer says that his work was "miraculously inspired" during those years, and that "books that were far stronger than everything that had gone before...came from his hand" during that time. Hugo's reaction? "Why was I not exiled sooner?"

C. S. Lewis gave this fascinating title to his autobiography: *Surprised By Joy*. Every believer who has long sought to walk with

Christ could borrow his title to describe features of his own life. One of the most potent elements in human life is that of surprise, whether sad surprise or happy surprise. God certainly knows the power of surprise, for after all, He built it into life. We may safely say that God delights to surprise and astonish His people in many ways.

A young soldier in the Civil War received wounds that left him very severely disabled for the rest of his life. He agonized over the reality of his dilemma, wrestling with the problem and with God. Near the end of his life, he wrote these insightful lines: "I asked for strength that I might achieve, and I was made weak that I might obey. I asked for health that I might do greater things; I was given infirmity that I might do better things. I asked for riches that I might be happy; I was given poverty that I might be wise. I asked for power that I might have the praise of men; I was given weakness that I might feel the need of God. I asked for all things that I might enjoy life; I was given life that I might enjoy all things. I have received nothing I asked for and all that I hoped for. My prayer is answered." His words exemplify the sentiment of Lena Ford in her poem, "Keep the Home Fires Burning," when she wrote, "There's a silver lining, Through the dark clouds shining."

Helen Keller suffered an illness at eighteen months which left her completely blind and deaf. For five years she was "imprisoned in a tomb of darkness and silence," to use her own words. Then with the help of Anne Sullivan, she fought back against her handicap. She later wrote, "The marvelous richness of human experience would have lost something of rewarding joy if there were no limitations to overcome. The hilltop hour would not be half so wonderful if there were not dark valleys to traverse."

Hear the incredible testimony of another champion of the Cross. Some of the most precious hymns ever written came from the pen of Fanny Crosby. Many worldly-wise people would call her blindness a waste and a tragedy, but (as true champions of the Cross always do) she had an entirely different perspective: "I have heard that the physician who unwittingly caused my blindness has never ceased expressing his regret at the occurrence, and that it is one of the sorrows of his life. But if I could meet him now, I would say, 'Thank you, thank you, over and over again, for making me blind.' Although it may have been a blunder on the physician's part, it was no mistake on God's. I verily believe it was His intention that I should live my days in physical darkness, so as to be better prepared to sing His praises and incite others to do so."

The greatest surprise of all of God's great surprises is the great Gospel surprise: A Baby in a Manger, a Man on a Cross, a Body in a Tomb, a Third-day Footrace, an Invincible Church, a March through History, and a Throne in Heaven — and sin lying writhing on the ground in death agony, Satan coiling like a serpent around the shaft of a Cross that has been driven through his vitals, and the saints of the church militant on earth tuning up to sing forever with the saints of the church triumphant in Heaven. I wonder what new surprise God holds today — just around the corner.

Chapter 5

A Prisoner's Passion

> *Some indeed preach Christ even of envy and strife; and some also of good will: The one preach Christ of contention, not sincerely, supposing to add affliction to my bonds: But the other of love, knowing that I am set for the defense of the gospel. What then? Notwithstanding, every way, whether in pretense, or in truth, Christ is preached; and I therein do rejoice, yea, and will rejoice. For I know that this shall turn to my salvation through your prayer, and the supply of the Spirit of Jesus Christ, According to my earnest expectation and my hope, that in nothing I shall be ashamed, but that with all boldness, as always, so now also Christ shall be magnified in my body, whether it be by life, or by death. (Philippians 1:15-20)*

Our last study was entitled "God's Surprise Party for the Disciple-Maker" We might call the opening verses of this study, "A Disciple-Maker's Unhappy Surprises." There were supposed leaders in the church in Philippi who were preaching Christ out of envy and strife and contention, thinking that they were making things harder for Paul by doing so. Their motive was to add other hardships to his imprisonment (verses 15, 16). "Some indeed preach Christ even of envy and strife," Paul wrote. One of the always-present dangers to a minister of the Word is that of comparison and competitiveness.

Satan loves to set ministers subtly against each other by comparisons which cause either feelings of superiority or inferiority and an aftermath of jealousy and competitiveness. A Christ preached out of "envy," or of "strife," or of "contention," presents a lop-sided Christ, a misrepresented Christ. Whenever the Gospel is diluted with anything — whether works, unresolved sin, bad disposition, or bad relationships — it loses its power in proportion to its dilution. Christian, be very aware of this as you serve Christ. Whatever is in you mixes with the Gospel. The Gospel "conditions" the sharer of it, and the sharer of it "conditions" the Gospel.

I have visited beautiful Yellowstone National Park on two occasions. The first time I was there, I returned again and again to the geyser basin that contains the "Old Faithful" geyser. I watched the geyser erupt several times, and I walked slowly through the entire basin, thoroughly fascinated with what I saw. There are over fifty geysers in the basin, and all of them come from the same subterranean source which produces Old Faithful. However, though Old Faithful erupts over one hundred feet into the air, the next highest geyser erupts less than fifty feet, and most of them erupt considerably less than that. Some barely reach the surface of the ground, creating only a gurgling pool of water. Why? They all come from the same heated source under the ground, and they all rise with equal force, but one erupts over one hundred feet into the air, while the others do not rise to even half that height. Why? The answer is found in the shape and size of the geyser cone in each case. The cone or shaft of Old Faithful is straight and smooth, while the shafts of the other geysers are crooked and rough. So the force of the eruption is dissipated by striking back and forth against the walls of the crooked shaft. The force of Old Faithful's eruption is unimpeded, while the force of the eruption of all the others is diluted by the crooked path of the water's flow.

What a picture of the Gospel presentation through human beings! The word "righteous" suggests something straight, while the word "iniquity" suggests something crooked. To the degree to which your life is positionally and practically lined up with "God

Almighty's Straight," to that degree the Gospel will come through your life pure, undiluted, and powerful. But to the degree that distortion prevails in your life, to that degree the power and purity of the Gospel are forfeited. The force of Paul's life has penetrated the centuries and the hearts of millions, while the influence of those who preached Christ with impure motives has died away, and they are mentioned today only in infamy.

In verse 19, Paul indicates his steadfast confidence in Christ. When he says, "I know that this shall turn to my salvation," he is in no way referring to his eternal salvation. He is referring rather to the ongoing and continuous daily salvation that a Christian needs all the time. Paul indicates the means by which he knows this salvation will be effected in his daily life — "through your prayers, and the supply of the Spirit of Jesus Christ." The prayers of Christians and the power of God, acting in conjunction, are two of the means by which God's purposes are advanced. Note the word "supply" in referring to the Holy Spirit. The supply matches the demand. There is no run on this bank! Our needs will never exhaust this supply.

In verse 20, we get an inside look into Paul's unconquerable spirit. He states his spiritual ambition in this powerful phrase, "According to my earnest expectation and my hope." The word translated "expectation" is a gigantic word, a triple compound, one large word made of three smaller words. The word is basically, *"apokaradokia."* "Kara" is the word for "head;" "dokia" is the word for "looking;" and "apo" is a Greek preposition which means "away from." Thus, the word has in it the ideas of an uplifted head, an outstretched neck, and a far-away look. If we can conjure in our minds a person standing on tiptoe, looking for and expecting a certain outcome, we can appreciate this word. This is the word that is used in Romans 8:19 for the posture and expectation of the created world as it waits anxiously for the full revelation of Christians as sons and daughters of God.

J. B. Phillips captures it in his paraphrase: "The whole creation is on tiptoe to see the wonderful sight of the sons of God coming into their own." License your imagination; image that picture in your mind. All of creation is standing at attention, straining to anticipate "that one far-off Divine event toward which the whole creation moves." Christian, hold your head up and keep looking forward; we are in for something awfully big! Creation won't be surprised; it is waiting eagerly for it to happen. But sadly, most human creatures will be shocked — by their willful ignorance, their stupid unbelief, and their inability to get in on it at the end. Now, picture Paul standing on tiptoe in a jail cell, with a far-away look in his eyes and solid realism in his heart, stating his ambitions and intentions! Even from prison, while facing the possibility of imminent death, Paul looks out to the broad expanse of a vast future in Christ and with Him.

Verse twenty closes with a magnificent Christian motto, one which every Christian might adopt to eternal advantage. "Christ shall be magnified in my body, whether it be by life, or by death." We see in this great motto: The Master Motive of the Christian experience — "that Christ shall be magnified"; the Vital Vehicle of its expression — "in my body"; and the Complete Commitment that must be exercised if this motive is to be fully realized — "whether it be by life, or by death."

THE MASTER MOTIVE OF THE CHRISTIAN EXPERIENCE

First, *the master motive of the Christian experience:* "That Christ shall be magnified." The word translated "magnified" is *megaluno*. We should already be quite familiar with the "mega" prefix. It means "very large." The word *megaluno* means "to make very large," or "to make great," or "to make conspicuous." It is used in a figurative sense to mean "exalt" or "glorify," but the devotional meaning of the word itself should be widely explored. Paul was determined to "magnify" Christ — to enable others to see Jesus in a way they had never seen Him before. Paul wanted to make Jesus look great! Paul fully agreed with another great Christian motto, the one spoken by John the Baptist: "He (Jesus) must increase, but I must decrease" (John 3:30).

There are two ways to magnify anything. One is by the microscopic principle, the other is by the telescopic principle. The microscope makes small things appear large, and the telescope makes distant things appear near. So magnification changes the perspective and perception of the viewer. The Christian must magnify Jesus in both ways. Why? It is surely not because Jesus is little or distant! Indeed, God is not inside the universe; the universe is inside of God! Jesus is already infinitely large. And it surely is not because Jesus is a great distance away. He "fills all in all." He is omnipresent.

A young boy was going to church on a Sunday morning. A sceptic saw him, and thought to have some fun at the boy's expense. "Where you goin', son," he asked. "To church," the boy replied with some satisfaction. "Whatcha gonna do there," asked the unbeliever. "Worship God," the boy answered. "Son, I'll give you a shiny red apple if you can tell me where God is," said the antagonist. The boy shot back, "Mr., I'll give you a whole barrel of apples if you can tell me where God ain't!" Conclusion of argument. No, we don't magnify Christ microscopically because He is small, or telescopically because He is far away. But remember that magnification changes the perspective and perception of the viewer. In the natural thinking of every man, Jesus seems to be much smaller than He really is, and He seems to be far away, unreachable and unknowable. The microscope enlarges the apparently small so that the thing viewed can be seen clearly, and the telescope makes things that are distant to appear close so they can be seen in proper proportion. The microbe may be invisible because of smallness, but the microscope "blows it up" so that it may be clearly seen. The celestial body may be so distant as to be unnoticeable, but the telescope "enlarges" it so it may be locally seen in true proportion.

One of the master motives of the Christian life is that through the Christian's personality as God's instrument (whether microscope or telescope), Jesus Christ may be made appropriately great in the eyes of those who have never heard of Him and in the eyes of those who have only a poor conception of His glorious Person. Martin Luther said, "The Apostle Paul had three wishes, and they were all about Christ — that he might be found in Christ, that he might be with Christ, and that he might magnify Christ." It must be noted, however that neither the microscope nor the telescope invents the image which it presents. It merely makes conspicuous that which was already there. No Christian can add anything to the full-orbed glory of the Person of the Lord Jesus Christ, but he may be used to cause Jesus to be properly appreciated among men. "Perish all things, so that Christ be magnified!" was the memorable and commendable watchword of Lord Shaftesbury, the English nobleman. There is no purer desire than this; there is no motto for the Christian that should dominate his thoughts and actions more than this. The Psalmist said, "Oh, magnify the Lord with me, and let us exalt His Name together" (Psalm 34:3). What a rallying cry for a disciple-maker and for every disciple of Christ! The Psalmist makes the motion, and Paul seconds it; can we Christians not cast a unanimous ballot? Our "earnest expectation and hope is that... Christ shall be magnified."

Before departing this first point, I must make a few remarks about the passion for world impact that dominates a disciple-maker. It seems to me that the two principles of magnification may be applied to geographic presentation of Christ as well as philosophic presentation of Christ. Remember that microscopes enlarge small things to the point of visibility, and telescopes draw distant things near so they can be seen immediately in their true size. With regard to geography, the microscopic principle is more needed in the United States and the western world which have had historic Christian roots, while the telescopic principle is needed in those areas of the world where Christ has not been known. In the United States, Jesus is near but very small to multitudes of people, so the microscope is needed. The further removed the location is from the United States, the more the telescope is needed — Jesus is very distant, and needs to be brought into their perception so He appears up close as large as He really is. What an assignment! What a vocation! What a challenge to qualitative relational living!

THE VITAL VEHICLE FOR ITS EXPRESSION

Second, this verse reveals *the vital vehicle which must be used for the expression* of this master motive: *"That Christ shall be magnified in my body."* My body is to be the "lens" that makes an apparently "small Christ" look conspicuously big, and an apparently "far-away Christ" look conspicuously close. It is in my body that Christ lives. "Know ye not that Christ lives in you?" Anything that lives in me must live in my body. I am an inhabited person. I have been tenanted by the living Presence of Jesus Christ. I have another Occupant, another Operator, another Owner than myself living in my body. I am a transporter, a carrier, a vehicle for the containment — and conveyance — of Jesus Christ.

When Mary, the mother of Jesus, received the angel's announcement about the coming birth of Jesus, she exclaimed, "My soul doth magnify the Lord," but this was also true of her body. Here Paul identifies the body as the location and instrument of magnification of Jesus. Paul was writing from Rome to the Philippian believers whom he dearly loved, and earlier, he had written to the Romans the renowned words, "I beseech you, brethren ... that you present your bodies a living sacrifice" (Romans 12:1). The body is the necessary instrument of the soul and the spirit for all action toward others, and all influence of others. Amy Carmichael stated it quaintly but accurately when she said, "Souls are more or less securely fastened to bodies, and as you can"t get the souls out and deal with them separately, you have to take them both together." Paul established this truth in II Corinthians 4:10, when he declared that we Christians should be "always bearing about in the body the dying of the Lord Jesus, that the life also of Jesus might be made manifest in our body."

E. Stanley Jones showed his usual penetrating insight when he wrote, "I have often imagined a convention of bodies talking about the people who inhabit them. A body stands up and says, 'Oh my, the man who inhabits me doesn't know how to live. He is full of fears, resentments, self-centeredness and guilts. He ties me in knots, and then doses me with all sort of medicines which have no relationship with what is wrong with me. There is nothing wrong with me. He upsets my functioning. I wish he knew how to live.' Another body stands up and says, 'It's wonderful to live with the man I live with. He is rhythmical, harmonious, and adjusted. We get along famously together, and I do prodigious things for him. It's a joy to do it.'"

Now, change the figure just a bit and let your body talk about the Jesus Who lives within it. "It is such an adventure to be indwelt by such an occupant. He is merciful, but mysterious. He is powerful, but sometimes puzzling. He is not mere baggage or dead weight, but a dynamic person with clear purposes. I wonder if the kind of body I give to Him matches the kind of life He wants to live within it?" Or imagine Jesus verbally evaluating your body as His Temple. A paraphrase of Jones' paragraph might make a good statement of Jesus' evaluation of His confinement in you. "I co-inhabit this body with such a struggling person! How I want him to rest in Me and My performance in and for him. I want him to see his body as I see it — the Temple in which I dwell in order to exhibit my Presence in the community around the Temple. How he confines Me and contorts Me instead of communicating Me. But he is My opportunity and My project. As he continues to grow in grace, I will be magnified more and more in his body."

THE COMPLETE COMMITMENT THAT MUST BE EXERCISED

Finally, we see *the complete commitment that must be exercised* if this purpose is to be fully realized. It is "my earnest expectation and my hope ... that Christ shall be magnified in my body, whether it be by life or by death."

Paul wanted Christian fruitfulness while he was living. According to verses 22, 24 and 25, he did not know whether his present imprisonment would result in release and further fruitful ministry by living, or in death. But he was determined to maximize either possibility in a fully Christ-honoring way. The outcome of his trial before the Roman Emperor was entirely uncertain, but Paul's purpose was the same no matter what the outcome. If he lived in chains in a prison cell or in the liberty of a self-determined schedule, he wanted Christ to be magnified. If Paul were permitted to continue in this life, he would continue to witness for Christ, serve Him, and bring forth "fruit unto God." The course of his life was settled.

But Paul also wanted fulfilment when he died. "Whether it be by life or by death." I have known many Christians who clearly dedicated their lives to God, but I have known few who consciously dedicated their deaths to God. Years ago, I was summoned as a young pastor to the hospital bedside of a saintly woman who had just been told that she had terminal cancer. Without remorse, protest or panic, she calmly asked me to join her in dedicating her death to God as she had sought to dedicate her life to God. Her closing months of life here were radiantly filled with Jesus and testimony for Him. This, I think, is a part of what Paul means. I consciously dedicate my death to God so that Christ can be magnified by my death as well as by my life. Note that Paul's stated ambition was not to die easily, or peacefully, or without pain. Though these are perfectly natural desires for any thoughtful person, they are overshadowed by this magnificent master motive, that "Christ shall be magnified ... by (my) death."

How do people die, anyway? They die essentially as they have lived. Their life purpose and momentum establish direction and determination for their death. The time they have logged with Satan or with God will be reflected in their death. In the Bible, the rich man died unprepared — because that is the way he had lived (Luke 16). Judas died unfaithful --because that is the way he had lived. Ananias died unclean — because that is the way he had lived (Acts 5). Stephen died unafraid — because that is the way he had lived (Acts 7). And Paul died unafraid, unashamed, and unabashed — because that is the way he had lived.

Paul lived and died the philosophy which Charles Wesley later wrote about:

> *"Ready for all Thy perfect will,*
> *My acts of faith and love repeat,*
> *Till death Thy endless mercies seal,*
> *And make the sacrifice complete."*

Chapter 6

Christianity Condensed

"For to me to live is Christ, and to die is gain." (Philippians 1:21)

In twelve brief words, the Apostle Paul has summarized the Christian view of life and death. At different times I have used two different titles for this verse. One is "Christianity Condensed," the other is "The Simple Secret of the Christian Life." The verse is a compound sentence constructed by the combining of two smaller sentences. All the words in the sentence are monosyllables, or one-syllable words. You do not need to know the complicated language of theological jargon to live the life that wins. Here it is in twelve brief, one-syllable words. And nine of the twelve words have three letters or less! This means that this verse is the very apex of simplicity. Nothing could be simpler, yet nothing is more profound.

The two shorter sentences are separated by a comma. The sentence before the comma gives the Christian view of life, while the sentence after the comma gives the Christian view of death. There are three strong words in the verse, the words "me," "live," and "Christ." The middle term, "live," is defined in the union of the two other words, "me" and "Christ." When the two terms, "me" and "Christ" are brought into right relationship, I become "alive unto God." The human finds real life in union with the Divine. This is the only combination that truly deserves to be called "life." The word "life" stands defined in the equation of this verse.

However, in our foolish attempts to find life, we take other extremes and combine them, and we call the result "life." We sometimes say, "To me to live is money." Or, "to me to live is pleasure." Or, "to me to live is fame." But the New Testament answers each of these combinations with this verdict, "Thou hast a name that thou livest, and art dead." All other combinations fail. The equation is not accurate without the Biblical components. Life is the unique product of a unique union. Jesus said, "This is life eternal, that they may know Thee the only true God, and Jesus Christ Whom Thou hast sent" (John 17:3). This is the theological statement; our text is the practical statement. The word "know" in Jesus' statement is a present tense continuous verb, and may be translated, "go on knowing," or "be knowing." So eternal life is an ongoing relationship or union with God through Jesus Christ. Also, this verb "know" is the same word that is used in the old Septuagint or Greek version of the Old Testament for sexual intimacy. Thus, the Bible says that "Adam knew Eve his wife, and she conceived, and brought forth a son." So life is found in intimate, loving interaction between a human being and God. Paul's words echo the Biblical formula for life. "For to me to live is Christ, and to die is gain." Here is the simple secret of the Christian life — and yet, so profound!

THE CHRISTIAN LIFE IS DEEPLY PERSONAL

First, the verse indicates that the Christian life is *deeply personal*. "To me to live is Christ." The words, "to me," stand in the emphatic position in the sentence. It is obvious that Paul is making a statement of deep personal feelings and preferences here. Jesus Christ is only possessed personally in the life of a human being. If these words do not comprise my personal testimony, then I am not a Christian. Martin Luther said, "Every man must do his own believing, just as every man must do his own dying." And he added, "The most important words in the Bible are the personal possessive pronouns, my and mine."

The Bible says that "God so loved the world" (John 3:16). It says that "Christ loved the church" (Ephesians 5:25). But this would bring me no benefit if I could not say with Paul, "Christ loved me, and gave Himself for me" (Galatians 2:20). The Bible says that Jesus is the "Good Shepherd who gives His life for His sheep" (John 10:11). It says that He is the "Great Shepherd" (Hebrews 13:20). It says that He is the "Chief Shepherd" (I Peter 5:4). But this would bring me no benefit if I could not say with David, "The Lord is my shepherd" (Psalm 23:1).

A cartoon by syndicated cartoonist George Clark showed two women talking over a cup of coffee. One says, "I'm pleased as punch with my weight-watchers club. Last week, we collectively lost 143 pounds among us!" But then she added, "However, I'm sad to admit that none of it was mine personally!" So where was the accomplishment? Where was the victory? She was not a real part of the victory or the accomplishment. You see, dear friend, it is not enough to be closely associated with Christian people, Christian places, or Christian activities. You must know Christ personally.

A girl named Edith went to church every Sunday, though nobody else in the family attended. One Sunday, her mother met her at the front door as Edith returned home from church. Edith was smiling broadly. Her mother asked her what she was smiling about. "Mama, the preacher preached from a verse of the Bible that had my name in it!" Edith announced. "Really, what was the verse?" her mother asked. "Luke 15:2, 'This man (Jesus) receiveth sinners, and Edith with them!'" she answered triumphantly. Dear friend, unless you have seen the proposition of salvation addressed personally to you, unless you have received Christ personally, unless you have been born of God personally — unless you have heard your name as personally called by God as Edith did, you have never been saved.

Ruth Graham, wife of evangelist Billy Graham, could not believe that she was included in God's life. She struggled and struggled, trying to believe. She finally went to see a pastor with her problem of unbelief. He opened a Bible to Isaiah chapter 53 and directed her attention to verse four, "He was wounded for our transgressions and bruised for our iniquities; the chastisement of our peace was laid upon Him, and by His stripes we are healed." The pastor said to Ruth Graham, "I want you to put your finger on that verse and read it out loud, inserting your own name in place of the word, "our." She did so, and suddenly, God turned the lights on in her inner spirit. "He (Jesus) was wounded for Ruth's transgressions." She saw the truth clearly, and entered into her inheritance in Christ. Have you seen yourself as the personal object of God's love and God's search? Do you realize that Jesus died for you as if you were the only sinner who ever lived, or the only sinner who ever needed to be died for? The Christian life is deeply personal.

THE CHRISTIAN LIFE IS WONDERFULLY PRACTICAL

Second, the text indicates that the Christian life is *wonderfully practical*. Look at the second pair of words, "to live." "To me to live is Christ." Note that this is a verb, "to live," and not a noun, "life." The verb is the action word of our language. The New Testament is a book about life and living. If I were to ask you, What is the main theme of the New Testament, what would your answer be? Consider this before you lock in an answer. The words "life" and "live" are used over 1,000 times in the New Testament! This alone makes a strong case that the main theme of the New Testament is life and living. Remember that there are three strong words in our text, "me," "live," and "Christ." And remember that the word "live" is the word that is defined by the union of the other two words. Now, living is a very practical thing (!). Someone said, "The problem of living is that it is so daily." Exactly! And this is the genius of Christianity. It offers a concept that covers every moment of every day. Jesus said, "I am with you always." "I will never leave you, nor forsake you." If we walk (a practical word) with Him, He will make our lives majestic. However, it must be honestly said that if we don't walk with Him, He will make our lives miserable. You see, He is serious in His desire for relationship with the people He made for such a relationship.

A little boy was taking an elementary science exam at school. One question was, "What is salt?" He could not remember the chemical formula, sodium chloride, so finally he wrote, "Salt is the stuff that spoils the potatoes when you leave it out!" Well, Jesus is the One who spoils life — when you leave Him out. There is no maliciousness in the arrangement when you learn that you must breathe to maintain physical life, and there is no maliciousness when you are told that you must have a relationship with God through Christ to have eternal life. No threat, just fact.

The word is "live," not dream, or wish, or hope, or theorize. The Christian life is a continuing experience. Can you imagine anyone announcing, "I'm real tired right at this moment, so I'm going to stop living for two hours and get some rest, then I'll resume the living at the end of that time." No, when a person stops living, it tends to be permanent! I don't live off of moments of inspiration or spasms of faith. I don't just live for one hour and thirty minutes on Sundays, then go dead for the rest of the time. I live every moment of every day and every moment of every night. Even so, Christ is my life every moment of every day and every moment of every night. He doesn't live in me in spells and spurts and spasms.

Many people could be called "hypodermic saints," or "epidemic saints." When they get a "fix," an inoculation, of Christianity in a super-charged atmosphere, they excitedly vow that they will live for Jesus. Their roots are planted in the excitement of the moment rather than in Christ. The "epidemic saint" catches the high-fevered contagion of a meeting or a crusade or an infectious preacher, but he fades away as quickly as he started. He is a chocolate soldier who stays firm in a cool and comfortable place, but melts when the sun gets hot in an exposed place.

A true relationship with Jesus Christ means that every part of my life is affected at all times; every relationship in my life is involved at all times; every moment of my life is to be changed and transformed. Whatever living means to me anywhere and all the time — working or lounging at home, driving a car or a bus, walking along a sidewalk, shopping in a grocery or a mall, reading the Bible or a novel or a newspaper, banging a typewriter or answering a telephone, standing behind a counter or in a line — whether I am tired or in full strength, sick or well, happy or disappointed, whether it is Monday morning or Saturday night, "to me to live is Christ." The Christian life is wonderfully practical.

THE CHRISTIAN LIFE IS GLORIOUSLY POSSIBLE

Third, the Christian Life is *gloriously possible*. One word in the verse makes it possible. That word is "Christ." Paul did not say, "To me to live is to confess Christ," or, "to me to live is to be like Christ," or, "to me to live is to live for Christ," or, "to me to live is to pray to Christ," or, "to me to live is to serve Christ." These formulas sound wonderful, and are easy replacements for the real thing. No activity, or function, or attribute of the life must be mistaken for the life itself. Jesus Himself is the Source, the Secret, the Substance, and the Solution of the Christian life. Someone said, "Many people are trying to live the Christian life when they don't have The Life to live." No accouterment or accompaniment of the life is the life itself.

Captain Reginald Wallis said, "The greatest day of my Christian life was the day I discovered I could not live it, and God did not intend me to. Then, and then alone, was I willing to invite the Lord Jesus to live His own life in me." Some people say, "The Christian life is out for me. I just can't live it." I've got good news for you. You are dead right; you can't live it! And furthermore, you were never expected to live it as far as God is concerned. Let me say it reverently but firmly. God isn't so stupid as to demand perfection and then expect a thoroughly imperfect person like you to live it!

Billy Graham asked a young man, "Are you a Christian?" "Well, I'm trying to be," was the reply, a quite typical reply to such a question. Graham asked teasingly, "Ever try to be an elephant?" To depend on your own effort is to guarantee failure, but to defer by repentance and faith to Christ's exercise in you is to guarantee fulfilment and fruitfulness.

Pastor Stuart Briscoe was on a preaching mission on the Isle of Man. A lady came to him at the end of one of the services and said glumly, "Mr. Briscoe, I just don't know what is wrong with me...." Briscoe interrupted before she could go further and said, "Ma'am, are you a Christian? Do you know you are saved?" "Why, yes, she replied, but I just don't know what is wrong with me...." Briscoe interrupted again, and politely asked her, "Ma'am, tell me in the simplest terms what happened to you the day you were saved." She thought a moment and replied, *"Well, Jesus came into me."* He said, "Excuse me, would you repeat that?" "Jesus came into me," she answered. "Please say that again," he insisted. She said, "Jesus came into me." "Again," he said gently. "Jesus came into me," she said. You see, the staggering and stupendous reality of having the eternal Son of God, the Lord of glory, the King of all kings, living in her had never become a vital reality to her, and thus the Christian life was an impossible proposition.

Every Christian has a decisive line of demarcation driven through his life. He has a B.C. (Before Christ) and an A. D. (Anno Domini, "in the year of our Lord") life. He has a Then and a Now. In the B. C., or Then, time, he had to say, "To me to live is (his own name goes here)." "To me to live is Herb." "To me to live is George, or Joe, of Polly, or Sue." Then, by a glorious new birth, he became a Christian. This means that the center of gravity within him shifted from himself to Christ. Do not misunderstand this. The Christian life is not a circle with only one center, Christ. This would violate and destroy your personality. No, the Christ life is an ellipse with two possible centers, you and Christ. Now, "He must increase, but you (the self-centered, fleshly, competitive self) must decrease." As the false usurper, the selfish you, decreases, the true you, the you that you were meant to be, emerges under the administration of Christ's life.

So life is Someone Else! Life is Christ. Shortly after Malcolm Muggeridge, the renowned English journalist, became a Christian, he delivered a sermon in Queen's Cross Church, Aberdeen, Scotland, on Sunday, May 26, 1968. In that sermon, Muggeridge made this confession: "I may, I suppose, regard myself, or pass for being, a relatively successful man. People occasionally stare at me in the streets — that's fame. I can fairly easily earn enough to qualify for admission to the higher slopes of the Inland Revenue — that's success. Furnished with money and a little fame even the elderly, if they care to, may partake of trendy diversions— that's pleasure. It might happen once in a while that something I said or wrote was sufficiently heeded for me to persuade myself that it represented a serious impact on our time — that's fulfillment. Yet I say to you, and I beg you to believe, multiply these tiny triumphs by a million, add them all together, and they are nothing — less than nothing — a positive impediment — measured against one draught of that living water Christ offers to the spiritually thirsty — irrespective of who or what they are. What, I ask myself, does life hold, what is there in the works of time, in the past, now and to come, which could possibly be put in the balance against the refreshment of drinking that water?" Life is Someone Else!

In the early 1960s, the heroic Christian leader Martin Niemoller came to America on a speaking tour. Knowing of his experience under the Hitler regime in Germany and of his resistance to the Nazis, two reporters representing large city newspapers hurried to hear him, expecting a sensational discussion of those war years. Instead, Dr. Niemoller preached a warm, Christ-centered Gospel message and yet hardly mentioned his experiences in Nazi Germany. The two reporters left the church greatly disappointed. As they departed, one reporter was heard saying to the other, "Six years in a Nazi prison camp, and all he has to talk about is Jesus Christ!" Life is Someone Else!

When John Bunyan was saved, he wrote in his journal, "O, I thought, Christ! Christ! There was nothing but Christ that was now before my eyes! O Christ! O Christ! O Christ! My Lord and my Savior! O Christ! O Christ!" It is Christ Who "is made unto us wisdom, and righteousness, and sanctification, and redemption" (I Corinthians 1:30). Life is Someone Else!

And life is someone else. Note the subtle change, the necessary addition, that is made when a person truly knows Christ. There is not only a shift of the "center of gravity" within him from self to

Christ, but there is also a shift from self to other people. "You are my joy and my crown," Paul wrote to the Thessalonians (2:19-20). You are "my joy and crown," he wrote to the Philippians (4:1). This is the whole point of the Christian life. We become fulfilled and gratified and useful as the focus of our lives turns from ourselves to Christ and others. When the focus of our lives is on Christ, He actually serves us, and, in a reciprocal miracle, we serve Him. When the focus of our lives is on others, we serve them for Christ's sake. If we only relate to Christ without a resulting focus on others, the Christian life becomes self-centered and mystical, an exercise in personal piety alone. This exercise appears wonderful at first, but it is in reality merely another caricature of the real Christian life.

On the other hand, if we sympathetically seek to focus on others without the monitor of a live relationship with Christ, we become mere social contributors — and soon that deteriorates into mere friendship. If I focus on Christ and His Life, then my relationships with others are incredibly sanctified.

We must realize that Jesus does not impart life as something separate from Himself. He Himself is the life which He imparts. "The gift of God is eternal life through Jesus Christ our Lord." When we get Him, we get "It." "He who has the Son has life, but he who has not the Son of God has not life" (I John 5:12). He said, "I am the way, the truth, and the life; no man comes unto the Father but by Me" (John 14:6). We use this verse almost exclusively for evangelistic purposes, but it has a far more profound meaning than merely to say that Jesus is the only way to God and to heaven. After all, He said three things in the verse, not just one.

Explore the phrases, and let me interpret for a moment. He said, "I am the way" — that we might be *saved*. He said, "I am the truth"-- that we might be *sure of it* and *sensible about it*. And He said, "I am the life" — that we might be *satisfied just with Him*. One hundred percent of Christians have gotten into the way and been saved. But substantially less than one hundred percent of Christians are sure of their salvation and sensible about their relationship with Christ. So someone is tampering in our minds and hearts with the authority of Jesus, because the same Christ spoke both sentences. But if there is a large decrease of participation from the first sentence of the verse to the second part, just look at the third part.

"I am the life" — that we might be satisfied just with Jesus, that we might find our sufficiency only in Christ. How many Christians do you know who have impressed you that they are satisfied just with Jesus? This is a very difficult question to answer. The only way it could be practically tested would be to remove everything but Christ and see if the person is satisfied. When the Apostle Paul came to die, he said, "I have kept the faith." You see, the faith was about all that he had left! But because he had lived a Christ-centered life, he was satisfied and gratified. How many Christians do you know who appear to find their sufficiency in Christ? Do you think you know even one?

Now, think carefully of the implications of the fact that Life is Someone Else, that Life is Christ and Christ is Life. Paul's equation is that Life equals Christ, and Christ equals Life. This means that there is no true life from which Christ is absent. Remove Christ, and you have removed life. Insert Christ, and you have inserted life. This means also that for any Christian to know and understand himself, He must get to know Christ — personally, intimately, accurately, and well. Dear Christian, if you are to have an adequate and accurate sense of identity, you must get to know Christ — because He is your Life!

Now, it is just this fact that makes the Christian life gloriously possible. Sadly, most Christians still think they must live the life for Christ instead of allowing Him to live His own life in union with their personalities.

A father came home from work. He saw his son sprawled on the front lawn. "Do you want to play?" the father asked. "Naw, Dad, I'm too tired!" "Why are you so tired, son?" "I've been riding a horse all over the neighborhood," the boy said, pointing to his broomstick horse that was lying beside him on the lawn. "Son," his Dad said, "riding a horse shouldn't make you that tired." "I know, Dad, but when you ride this kind of horse, you have to do your own galloping." A Christian has the winged horse of the universe, Jesus the Son of God, to carry him, but sadly, most Christians still do their own galloping!

In happy contrast, consider the ride which Lucy and Susan enjoyed on Aslan after he had risen from the dead in C. S. Lewis' great story entitled *The Lion, the Witch, and the Wardrobe*. An incredible story of redemption from sin through death and resurrection, the story climaxes with the two girls commanded to get on Aslan's back and ride. "That ride was perhaps the most wonderful thing that happened to them in Narnia. And it was a ride on a mount that doesn't need to be guided and never grows tired. He rushes on and on, never missing his footing, never hesitating, threading his way with perfect skill ... "

To get the full meaning, do yourself a favor and read the entire book. Go back to your childhood for a little while, and enjoy the ride.

The Christian life is gloriously possible because Jesus communicates His Life to you and wants to carry you all the way home.

Every person on earth lives at all times in one of two verses from Paul's letter to the Philippians. The first is our text in Philippians 1:21: "To me to live is Christ." The other is one chapter away in Philippians 2:21: "For all seek their own, not the things which are Jesus Christ's."

> *"Only two philosophies occupy life's shelf,*
> *Either live for Christ, or live for self."*

Those two philosophies of life, that of the Savior and that of Satan, confront us in these two verses. Everlasting life is life with Christ at its center, but the other philosophy, that of self-serving, created Satan and agrees with him — and the person who lives that way will have to endure Satan's company forever! Let's finally consider the permanent consequences of the Christ-centered life.

THE CHRISTIAN LIFE IS ETERNALLY PROFITABLE

When a person says, "To me to live is Christ," he will enjoy Christ's company forever. The Christian life is *eternally profitable.* "To me to live is Christ, and to die is gain." A Christian can live or he can die — but he cannot lose! The word translated "gain" in this verse is "kerdos," which means gain in the sense of "profit." It was used often in the secular writing of Paul's day to refer to interest gained on invested money. In II Timothy 1:12, Paul spoke of his faith as a deposit (the KJV translates it "commit") of his whole life into Christ's keeping. According to Colossians 3:3 and other Scriptures, this means that Paul's whole destiny went into Heaven's triple-padlocked Safety Deposit Box. We often call this Eternal Security, and it is exactly that. But it is not a mere sterile idea; it is part of a dynamic relationship.

You see, the only person who can give Paul's analysis of death is the person who is living out Paul's analysis of life. Only the person who can truthfully say, "To me to live is Christ," can fully, accurately and faithfully say, "And to die is gain." If a person belongs to Christ in life, he will also belong to Christ in death, and there is victory either way. The Moffatt translation says, "Death means gain." If Christ is my life, then death must be "gain," because it simply means that I get much, much more of what I was living for — Christ! When the time came for Paul to die — he was beheaded near Rome, according to history — you might have said to him, "Do you see the Emperor's executioner approaching?" Paul might have answered, "No, but I see Christ!"

Death meant just one thing to Paul, and that was a complete and unhampered union with Jesus. Paul talked freely, naturally and realistically about death. He called it "the last enemy," because it is just that. Paul never denied its stark reality, nor did he evade its imminence. It is a sure sign of our carnal-mindedness, immaturity, and insecurity that we moderns do not talk of death except in hush-hush voice or in somber tone and tragic mood. Or we swing to the other extreme, the "Polyanna" mood of denial, deliberately acting as if we are invincible or that we will face the dark "king of terrors" only when he gallops across our path. Meanwhile, "eat, drink, and be merry" is our mediocre lifestyle. But Paul not only talked freely and naturally about death; he actually looked forward eagerly to the experience. He knew that death was the limousine that would transport him into the King's Presence, and though the last few miles of the ride might be very rough and bumpy, that "it will be worth it all, when we see Jesus!"

It is the clear teaching of Scripture that death has two sides to it, and not just one. For example, Jesus spoke of death as "sleep," and sleep has wakefulness both before and after it. Death is an "exodus," and we cannot imagine an exodus from one place without an entrance into another. Death has a before and an after, and one Person holds the key to victory in the life before death and in the life after death. In the context of verse 21, our text uses a large and expansive word for death. In verse 23, it is referred to as a "departure." Paul said, "I have a desire to depart and be with Christ, which is far better." He pictures himself as occupying a "narrow place", like a man walking down a narrow corridor between two solid walls. Paul is between two "pulls," one outward toward his earthly companions, the other upward toward Heaven. He says, "My preference, my desire, is to depart and be with Christ." That is the "gain" of death to a Christian.

The word "depart" (verse 23) is another of those treasure-packed words of Scripture. In Paul's day, it was often used as a soldier's term, and it meant to take down a tent — to loosen and remove the pegs, to fold up the fabric, to break camp and to prepare to move to a new location. II Corinthians 5:1 says, "We (Christians) know, that if our earthly house of this tabernacle (portable tent) be dissolved (the work death does), we have a building of God, a house (a permanent residence, unlike a portable tent) not made with hands, eternal in the heavens."

Then the word "depart" is a sailor's term, and it meant to loosen the cables and set sail. Think of it. A ship is moored at dockside in a harbor. Then it loosens its moorings and moves out to the threat and the adventure and the prospect of the high seas.

Friends and loved ones in the harbor might weep over the departing passengers and say, "Farewell." But a while later, in a distant harbor, other friends and relatives might smile as they hear the cry, "Ship ahoy!" and a few minutes later, the passengers will receive warm and wonderful welcomes from those who greet them in the new land. So is death to a Christian.

The word "depart" is also a sojourner's word, and it simply means to move from one location to another. You see, when a Christian dies, he only changes location, he does not change companionship. Who is going to heaven? Those who live in a vital relationship with Christ on earth; those who can validly say, "To me to live is Christ."

If we are to adequately explore the phrase, "and to die is gain," we must at least briefly inventory the Christian's "Death Benefits." In what sense is it true for a Christian to say, "To me... to die is gain"?

Death is gain for a Christian, first, because it will mean *eternal freedom from the problems of life*. As incredible as it may seem, there is coming a time (an eternity!) for a Christian when he will never sin again, never suffer again, and never struggle again! "To die is gain."

Second, death is gain for a Christian because it will mean an *eternal future in a place*. Jesus said to His disciples, "I go to prepare a place for you." Note the words "prepare" and "place," and remind yourself that Jesus was a carpenter while here on earth. As of this writing, He has been in Heaven for about 2,000 years — and possibly He has done a considerable amount of interior decorating on the place — "for you"! If the language used to describe it in Revelation 21 and 22 is literal language, then it is unbelievably beautiful. If the language is figurative, then the place itself is even more beautiful than figurative language can describe.

Two Christian men died together and entered heaven together. As they were touring the premises, one exclaimed, "Man! This place is spectacular! Why didn't someone tell us in advance how beautiful it was?" The other excitedly replied, "And just think of it! We could have been here ten years sooner if we hadn't eaten all those health foods!" Forgive the facetiousness, but this is something to laugh about and to celebrate. When the prospect has materialized into reality, you may be sure that we will laugh and shout and sing and celebrate — and I am sure there will be enough fuel for our celebration to last forever!

Finally, death is gain for a Christian because it will mark the beginning of unhindered *eternal fellowship with a Person*. Jesus said, "I go to prepare a place for you, that where I am, there you may be also." In His great high priestly prayer in John 17, Jesus prayed, "Father, I will that they also, whom You have given to me, be with me where I am."

A dentist had an upstairs office. One day, he was working on a patient in the dental chair. Suddenly, they both heard a loud scratching sound at the door. The dentist laughed as he explained, "That's my dog. I left him downstairs. He has never been in this room; he doesn't even know that it would be a safe place. But he knows that I am here, and he just wants to be with me." It might greatly impress some people to be told that the streets of heaven are made of gold, the walls of jasper, and the gates of pearl. But when a person has lived by this standard, "To me to live is Christ," he would have only one criterion in evaluating heaven: "Forget the furniture of the place, and its location. I want to know one thing: *Is Jesus there?*"

> *"My knowledge of that place is small*
> *The eye of faith is dim;*
> *But it is enough that Christ knows all*
> *And I shall be with Him."*

I want to ask you, dear friend, to finish my sermon for me. The method will be simple. Dare to write out your life philosophy in an honest sentence. If someone were to ask you, "In a word, what are you living for?" what would you say? In a word, what is your dominant aim or motive in life? Perhaps you would have to reply, "To me to live is money." Or, "to me to live is pleasure." Or, "to me to live is fame." Or perhaps your philosophy would be the all-inclusive one, "To me to live is self." Now, dare to finish the sentence of Philippians 1:21: "And to die is ... " If you must admit that life to you is summarized in a quest for money, then to die is certainly not gain; it is rather loss, because you can't take it with you. Billy Sunday added, "And if you could, it would melt where you are going!" If life for you is summarized as a quest for pleasure, then to die is loss, because God will not cater to your selfish appetites, sensations, and thrills. Any other motive will end up holding the same loss!

The only person who can say, "To me ... to die is gain," is the person who has happily adopted this lifestyle, "To me to live is Christ." You see, dear friend, "Heaven holds all of that for which you sigh," but it is only yours if you can say, "To me to live is Christ." If Christ is your very life now, He will be your very life forever. "Do you not see that executioner, Paul?" "No, I see no executioner." "Then what do you see?" "Ever and always, I see only Christ."

Chapter 7

Earmarks of a Disciple-Maker

Only let your conversation be as it becometh the gospel of Christ; that whether I come and see you, or else be absent, I may hear of your affairs, that ye stand fast in one spirit, with one mind striving together for the faith of the gospel; And in nothing terrified by your adversaries: which is to them an evident token of perdition, but to you of salvation, and that of God. For unto you it is given in the behalf of Christ, not only to believe on him, but also to suffer for his sake; Having the same conflict which ye saw in me, and now hear to be in me. (Philippians 1:27-30; King James Version)

Only, let your conduct be worthy of the gospel of Christ, so that whether I come and see you for myself or hear about you from a distance, I may know that you are standing firm, one in spirit, one in mind, contending as one man for the gospel faith, meeting your opponents without so much as a tremor. This is a true sign to them that their doom is sealed, but a sign of your salvation, and one afforded by God himself; for you have been granted the privilege not only of believing in Christ but also of suffering for him. You and I are engaged in the same contest; you saw me in it once, and, as you hear, I am in it still. (Philippians 1:27-30; New English Bible)

Paul was writing to common Christians, not superstar saints. He was writing to frontline troops in the trenches, not "stain-glass saints wearing haloes and enshrined in a cathedral."

Philip Yancey, a widely read Christian author, places Christians into two categories. Perhaps the categories are a bit strained and unfair, but we can still learn valuable lessons from his analysis. Yancey says that there are Christian entertainers and Christian servants. He identifies the entertainers as the high-profile leaders who fill the Christian periodicals, dominate Christian conferences, conventions, and seminars, and appear on our television screens. They have fame, prestige, and money. On the other hand, the servants are seldom in the spotlight. They work steadily and faithfully without fanfare, and often in remote places. They often live among the rejects of society and work for long hours at low pay and with no applause. Their talents and skills are given to the poor and uneducated. Though the discernment of these categories can be too rigid, I believe the Bible supports Yancey's assessment.

One of my favorite writers is the late Cambridge scholar, C. S. Lewis. In almost all of his Christian works, Christians are seen in aprons and overalls, not in clergy gowns or choir robes. For example, in his classic work, *The Great Divorce*, a great and noble lady is being drawn in a chariot on the streets of heaven. However, the dreamer who is reporting the story discovers that it is "only Sally Smith, a charwoman of Golders Green." The charwoman is seen in her true character and nobility in heaven, though she was a "commoner" on earth. In *The Magician's Nephew*, another classic from the *"Chronicles of Narnia"* series, a common Cockney cab-driver from London is seen to be the Adam figure of the story — and a "High King," at that! During his life in London, he had been a man of simple faith in Christ, cheerfulness and trustworthiness of disposition, and had been "kind to his horse and loving to his wife." You see, in Heaven, faith, joy, kindness and love are the stuff royalty is made of — though it may have traveled in disguise as a cab-driver on earth. In another of Lewis' classics, *That Hideous Strength*, a group of simple believing women are choosing gowns at St. Anne's. As each one tries on her gown, we see her suddenly transfigured and revealed gloriously for what she really is. When all the returns are in, it will likely be the "troops in the trenches," not the preachers in the pulpits, who will receive the special awards. It is to these troops that Paul addresses our text. He is thinking like a disciple-maker — and why not, for that's what he is! He is thinking of them as disciples — "Christ's Pupils and God's Harvest Hands." As he combines his disciple-building mentality with their disciple-being responsibility, he presents to us a great list of "the earmarks of a disciple-maker." Let's examine them.

A COMPASSIONATE CONCERN

Every disciple-maker is consistently dominated by a *compassionate concern* which governs his life and actions. It is suggested in our text by the use of two words of contrast, the words "perdition" and "salvation" (vs. 28). A true disciple-maker is consistently conscious of the realities of an eternal hell and an eternal heaven. He knows that there is "a hell to avoid, and a heaven to gain."

The word "perdition" describes the eternal condition after death in which an unbeliever will live forever. Dr. Thayer defined it as "the destruction which consists in the loss of eternal life, in eternal misery." Perdition is the final, eternal, irrevocable ruin of a person without Christ. In the Bible, the word never means annihilation, or the cessation of existence.

The other word, "salvation," includes both a crisis of rescue and a process of continuing safety. The one-time crisis of salvation is the great and gracious rescue of a sinner from the penalty and condemnation of his sins. This rescue is accomplished by God objectively through the Death and Resurrection of Jesus Christ, and subjectively through the new birth, a miracle of conviction and conversion which "unselfs" the sinner and "re-centers" his life in Christ. The ongoing process is the progressive sanctifying of the believer, securing a condition of permanent safety in Christ and a conduct of saintliness and service. The process includes the continual cleansing of sin (I John 1:7), continual child-training for God's sons and daughters, and continual commitment to service. This salvation already belongs to every person who has received and trusted Christ, but it reaches its glorious consummation in the future in heaven.

Perdition and salvation are two radically different conditions. Someone said it like this: "There is a difference between running a race and walking off a gangplank." Most people who think they are running a race are actually walking off a gangplank. The person who is truly running the race has signed on with Jesus Christ, the Greatest of Coaches, taken the Coach's Training, and is on his way to heaven, but the other person is merely marking time to stay out of hell. The disciple-maker must live at the place of uneasy tension — acknowledging heaven and hell and bringing others to face them as well.

My wife, Judy, and I are presently reading a book together in an early morning reading time. The book is entitled *Heroes*. It tells the stories of twenty believers, ten great Christian women and ten great Christian men. We recently read the chapter on Amy Carmichael, the great missionary of Dohnavur Fellowship in India. This paragraph describes the great spiritual crisis of her life:

"When she was seventeen, seeing on the street in Belfast a poor woman in rags, carrying a heavy bundle, she had what amounted almost to a vision of the things that really matter in life. She and her two brothers, moved with pity for the poor soul, helped her along, though they were embarrassed to be seen with her. Amy described it as a horrid moment, for they were 'not at all exalted Christians,' but on they plodded through the gray drizzle. Suddenly words came to her, 'Gold, silver, precious stones, wood, hay, stubble . . . the fire shall try every man's work of what sort it is. If any man's work abide . . .' From that moment, for the rest of her life, it was eternal things that mattered."

Happy is the disciple-maker who has been brought by the quickening work of God in his spirit to the point that he lives in light of eternity. He will not see people merely "after the flesh," but rather against the foil of eternal destinies in the making. He will warn those who are in danger of hell, seek to win them to Christ, and work to build those who are won to live in obedience to Jesus and to win others. He will also be aware that he lives in a position of creative tension, and he will pass this redemptive tension on to others. Those who sound warnings and assist in rescues are not leisure-oriented people, and they are often labeled "alarmists" by their society. But remember, history now recognizes Paul Revere as a hero — though he disturbed everybody's sleep on that fateful night! If a ship is sinking, the passenger's best friend is the one who urges him to the lifeboat.

Years ago, I heard an evangelist preach on the subject, "Hell Is No Joke," and he certainly was right. However, I recently saw a tee-shirt whose picture and logos humorously enforced the serious realities of heaven and hell. The picture on the shirt showed Satan leering with a wide grin as he holds a knife in one hand and a fork in the other. Flames are leaping from a big fire beneath him. He is apparently enjoying roasting a sinner in hell. Underneath is this pointed question: "Wouldn't you really rather hear JESUS say, Well Done?"

Suppose that you work as a cook in a restaurant. One day, when the restaurant is crowded with noonday customers, a fire breaks out in the kitchen and is quickly out of control. In the dining room, everyone is relaxed, having a good time, and eating a good lunch. The fire forces you into a very unhappy task. You must interrupt and disturb those happy and contented customers. You must secure quick and decisive action from them, a matter of life and death. But they have no idea of the seriousness of the situation. Either you must abandon them to their fate and bear the guilt of inaction, or you must risk their resentment and protest. They do not want to be interrupted. The waitresses out front don't want to miss their tips. The owner doesn't want a negative image. But you have a message that will save their lives, even though it makes them extremely uncomfortable at the moment.

With this awesome responsibility in mind, the disciple-maker invests his life redemptively in the lives of others. He is not likely to be appreciated by society at large, and may even be depreciated by many inside the restaurant (!), but the ultimate realities dominate his life, anyway. He is consistently governed by a compassionate concern.

A CONSUMING COMMITMENT

The disciple-maker is marked by a *commitment that consumes* his thoughts, his time, his talents, his energy, his schedule, and his efforts. Eugene Peterson paraphrases verse 27 in this manner: "(Be) singular in vision, contending for people's trust in the Message." "Contending for people's trust in the Message." This should be the commitment of every Christian's life, but it is certainly essential in the life of a disciple-maker. There is a military metaphor pursued in this great passage of Scripture, an atmosphere of war. Here, the Gospel flag is placed in the hands of the common Christian soldier, and the goal is the same always — to plant the flag in other lands and in other lives. The word, "contending," is by no means too strong a word for this activity. It conjures such ideas as tension, opposition, competition and conflict. The ground will be heavily contested by the enemy every step of the way. The Christian must challenge the enemy in the fellowship — and outside. In the fortress — and outside. In the foxhole — and beyond. When Jesus said, "The gates of hell shall not prevail against my church," He was not picturing His Church in a "holding" posture, a defensive stance. Gates are defensive devices. The church is on the march, assaulting the very defenses of hell. And it will win! "The gates of hell shall not prevail against it." However, the army still must train, discipline itself, and attack. Every front is strategic, every battle will be strenuous, and every Christian is crucial. The true soldier knows that there is no gain without pain, no blessing without bleeding. Horatius Bonar stated it well in these poetic lines:

"Go, labor on while it is day,
The world's dark night is hastening on;
Speed, speed thy work; cast laziness away;
Only with strong wrestlings are souls won."

Note Paul's emphasis on the independent duty of believers. He says, "Whether I come and see you, or else be absent, you stand fast in one spirit, with one mind striving together for the faith of the gospel." American Christianity tends to be a leader-oriented, leader-dependent, hero-elevating kind of Christianity. This tends toward a paternalistic spirit, which is altogether too widespread in the community of faith — baby believers hanging on to the coattails or apron strings of a victorious saint, and the leader in turn building his image of success on the number of such followers who cling to him. Great wisdom is needed here. It is wonderful to have good leaders, and they should be duly honored and recognized. But you must not depend too much on them. As usual, the key is balance. Your dependence is to be upon Christ, not on any Christian. If you are to be a faithful disciple-maker, both dependence and independence (and inter-dependence) will mark your life. Soldiers may get cut off from their commanding officers, and still should fight with efficiency and ability. A disciple should have a great measure of wholesome independence before God, as well as wholesome interdependence on his fellow believers. He should be independent enough to be a self-starter for Christ and to be an efficient producer even if he stands alone. He should represent his commanding officer and his country well, even if he fights alone.

The disciple-maker will think with this military mentality, and will train the disciples God gives him to think in this manner, also. He will do everything he can do to master the disciplines that will enable him to advance the Gospel — the discipline of evangelistic strategy and technique, the discipline of Christian apologetics, the discipline of relational living, the discipline of teamwork and the discipline of wise planning and training. He will be consumed by the commitment to "contend for people's trust in the Message."

CONSISTENT CONDUCT

The third earmark which a disciple-maker will reveal is *consistency of conduct* in his daily life. Verse 27 says, "Let your conduct be worthy of the Gospel of Christ." Let it be such as "becometh the Gospel," the King James Version says. One woman says to another, "That dress becomes you," and we recognize that she is pointing out a match between person and apparel. There is to be a becoming match of Christian and Gospel so that the Christian adorns the Gospel. The Christian is responsible to let the world see the beauty of the Gospel by the quality of his life. Each Christian should be very careful that his behavior doesn't clash with the basic beliefs of the Gospel. Paul indicated that there are some practices that should "not be once named among you, as becometh saints" (Ephesians 5:3).

Paul uses a rather puzzling word for "conduct" in this verse. It is worth our time to try to solve the puzzle. The Greek word is "politeuesthe," the word from which we get our words, "polity, politics, policeman," etc. The word literally means "citizenship." It refers to our duty because we are members of a certain group. As Christians, we have both individual and corporate duties. We are individual believers, but it is impossible to function as a true Christian with an independent spirit. The moment a believer is saved, he is incorporated into Christ's body, and his relationship thereafter is the same as one member of his body to all the other members. Fingers and toes do not act independently of the body of which they are a part, and no Christian should act independently of the fellowship in which God has placed him. Your position in Christ and His Body brings you unbelievable resources and privileges, but it also entails great responsibilities and duties.

There is an internationally used French expression that presents this idea. "Noblesse oblige," they say. "Rank imposes obligation, privilege brings responsibility," is the meaning of the phrase. Notable rank requires honorable conduct. Jesus said it first: "Unto whomsoever much is given, of him shall be much required" (Luke 12:48). Remind yourself that the Philippians were Roman citizens because Philippi was a Roman colony. As Roman citizens, they enjoyed special privileges, but these privileges entailed special responsibilities, also. So, too, Christians are an outpost of heaven's citizens on earth (Philippians 3:20), and their entire demeanor should be a miniature reflection of their true homeland.

The word translated "worthy of" carries the idea of weight. In fact, the idea is that of equal weight. Picture an old set of scales with a center pole and a crossbar. At each end of the crossbar is a pan in which objects are placed to be weighed. In Paul's illustration, one pan contains the glorious and weighty Gospel of Christ. The other pan holds your life. The startling fact presented here is that your life is to be of equal weight to the claims and expectations of the Gospel. "Who is equal to such a task?" It is easy to see that the Christian needs daily discipline, daily vocation, and daily miracles to live the Christian life. Only then will his conduct be consistent with the glorious realities and claims of the Gospel of Christ.

CONSTANT COOPERATION

The fourth mark of a disciple-maker is *constant cooperation* with other believers. "All of you are to stand fast in one spirit, with one mind striving together for the faith of the Gospel" (verse 27). The word "together" translates the Greek preposition "sun," which is equivalent to our English prefix, "co-," as in such words as "cooperate," which means "to operate together." A "co-partner" is a partner together with someone else. The preposition "sun" is used 16 times in Philippians in conjunction with verbs, showing Paul's emphasis upon teamwork and cooperation. The word translated "striving together" is the word "sunathleo." The root word gives us our English words "athlete" and "athletics." But the prefix "sun" lets us know that Paul is not thinking of sports that require only individual participation, such as boxing, singles tennis, golf, etc. Rather, he is thinking of team participation in which success depends largely on standing together and being united.

When Lefty Gomez, the Hall of Fame baseball pitcher, was asked the secret of his success as a pitcher, he replied, "Clean living and a fast outfield." He knew that any participant in team sports is only as good as the team that supports him. In the same manner, a disciple-maker is only as good as the team that supports him. How many times have I been made to look far better than I really am because of the great disciples God has graciously given to me. A disciple-maker should be a relational person, always looking for and cultivating relationships for Christ's sake. John Wesley said, "There is no such thing as a solitary saint." He was right. If a burning coal is isolated, it will burn out quickly, but in a fire of many coals, it will burn long and bright.

Two books with similar settings are <u>Robinson Crusoe</u> and <u>Swiss Family Robinson</u> (I call them the "Robinson books"). Both tell of the efforts of survivors of shipwrecks at sea to maintain their lives on lonely islands. The obvious difference, however, is that Robinson Crusoe was alone while the others were a family. There is an analogy here to the Christian, and especially to the disciple-maker. No disciple-maker should be a Robinson Crusoe struggling alone against fear and loneliness on an isolated island of individual faith. If he remains alone for very long, he should check his vision, his understanding of the disciple-making process, his availability to the Holy Spirit to make disciples, and his relational aptitudes with other people. These are areas of deficiency where the disciple-making process may break down in an individual's life. Every disciple-maker should be more like an active, aggressive, functional, contributing member of Swiss Family Robinson — dependent on a close, vital family relationship to survive and be productive in a hostile environment. Paul's words clearly reveal his conviction that there is great power in relationships, cooperation and teamwork — the very ingredients that are at the heart of the disciple-making process.

Permit a personal testimony at this point. I have traveled to many foreign lands to teach national pastors and leaders how to fulfill the Great Commission by building world-visionary, world-impacting, multiplying disciples. Sometimes (usually because schedule has not permitted time to enlist a team) I have traveled alone. The efficiency reduces greatly when I am alone, the temptations are much greater to be slack and indulgent, the drain is much more obvious, and the process is left without a visual example. However, when I have at least one other disciple/trainer with me, all of these problems are resolved. Some of the greatest men I have ever known on earth have attended me on many of these trips, and the transfer of truth to life-changing reality is always much greater when they are with me. How I thank God for them, and I pray earnestly that God will give them the same great privileges that He has given me. Disciple-making is marked by the absolute necessity of constant cooperation with a large network of other disciples and disciple-makers.

CONSPICUOUS COURAGE

The last mark of a disciple-maker which I see in this text is *conspicuous courage* in standing for Christ and with other Christians. This entire passage of Scripture reveals the great need for conspicuous courage in the Christian community. No disciple-maker can afford to be without a Spirit-produced courage, a spiritual boldness, in being a disciple, in building disciples, and in leading disciples. Such terms as "stand fast," "striving together," "conflict," "in nothing terrified by your adversaries," highlight the need for courage. If anybody ever exhibited and exemplified courage, it was surely the Apostle Paul.

Samuel Johnson wrote of courage, "Unless a man has the virtue of courage, he has no security for preserving any other virtue." In the Bible, courage has less to do with macho strength and more to do with heart and character. In fact, in the French language, the word "corage" means "heart." "Lift up your hearts, be of good courage," the Bible says. Henry Van Dyke said, "Courage is the soul's standing army, which negatively keeps it from conquest, pillage and slavery, and positively guarantees its advance and victory."

J. M. Barrie, author of the child's fantasy, Peter Pan, was giving a convocation address at Saint Andrews Church. He held up a tattered letter written to him from Captain Scott, the explorer who died exploring the South Pole. It was discovered on his frozen body and sent to Mr. Barrie. Listen to a segment of the letter:

"Hoping this letter may be found and sent to you. I write you a word of farewell....Goodbye — I am not at all afraid of the end, but sad to miss many a simple pleasure I had planned. We are in a desperate state — feet frozen, etc., no fuel, and a long way from food, but it would do your heart good to be in our tent to hear our songs and our cheery conversation. We are very near the end.... We did intend to finish ourselves when things proved like this, but we have decided to die naturally."

Paul calls for this kind of singing, triumphant courage in our text. He himself exemplified it, and felt confident in inviting others to reveal it as well. The term "striving together" is an invitation to show a common courage in advancing the Gospel. Philippi was named after Philip of Macedon, the father of Alexander the Great. Philip was the one who first used the military strategy known as the "phalanx," the formation of a solid front of soldiers advancing upon an enemy. The need for courage was equal and common on such a front. The same is true in the community of faith.

"In nothing terrified by your enemies," Paul says. Commentator R. P. Marting says, "'Terrified' is a strong term, unique in the Greek Bible, and denotes the uncontrollable stampede of startled horses." Use your imagination. See a startled horse shying at something which is only half seen, or which is mistaken for something else. The horse is thrown into sudden confusion, and then into possibility of accident or disaster. This is especially meaningful to me just now because my wife, an accomplished rider, was riding with a friend some months ago when their horses were suddenly "spooked" by the intrusion of other unexpected horses. Their horses broke into a wild gallop and both ladies were thrown from their horses. Fortunately, they both escaped with only severe bruises. This is Paul's illustration in verse 28. As we journey along the road of life, we may encounter threatening circumstances which may break up our serenity and throw us into panic. This may cause us to shy from our appointed course, and might even cause moral or spiritual disaster. Because of fear, we may lose our way. We need to be shored up with a store of courage.

In Bunyan's classic allegory, <u>Pilgrim's Progress,</u> Christian was climbing the Hill Difficulty. He saw two giant lions along the path, but he did not see the chains that bound them. The same may be true of us. We can see the menace, the peril, from far away, but we do not see the defensive grace God has provided until it is too late.

There is an old fable about a little boy who saw a witch turn herself into a cat. The cat began to run after the frightened little boy, who ran away as fast as he could. But when he turned around the cat had grown and become the size of a calf and was gaining on the boy. When he looked around again the cat had grown even more and was now the size of a house. The little boy ran with all the energy that he had. Finally he couldn't run anymore. There was nothing else to do but to turn and face the danger. So he turned toward the cat. The cat turned and ran and the boy began pursuing it. The farther it ran the smaller it became until finally it was small enough to scamper back into the witch's house. A fable full of truth! Courage will chase away the cat. Faith will overcome fear. In every situation, we must disregard our fears, trust God, and go forward. When we reach the lions, we will find that they are chained. To learn again from Pilgrim's Progress, there may be cold water on this side of the wall, but the oil of inexhaustible grace is sustaining the fire on the other side.

A Gospel illustration will help here. A shadowy form appeared to the Apostles on the water in a stormy night, and they were thrown into uncertainty and fear. They cried in panic, "It is a ghost!" And Jesus answered, "It is I, be not afraid!"

One summer night during a severe thunderstorm a mother was tucking her little boy into bed. She was about to turn the light out in his bedroom and close the door when she heard his trembling voice say, "Mommy, will you stay here with me tonight?" Mother walked back to his bed, gave him a big hug, and said tenderly, "I can't, son, I have to sleep in daddy's room." There was a moment of silence. Then in a shaky voice the little boy said, "The big sissy!"

The world needs Christians who are not chocolate soldiers, melting in fear before any enemy; it must see believers instead who will seek grace from God to "stand fast" to their purpose. Paul and Silas had modeled this courage at the time of the founding of the Philippian church when they had sung songs of praise in their jail cell at midnight A Christian must not be startled or stampeded by the enemies of the Gospel. "Having done all, he must stand."

These, then, are the marks of a disciple-maker. He is recognizable by a compassionate consideration that dominates his life — heaven and hell are real, and will last forever. He is marked by a consuming commitment — he is always "contending for people's trust in Christ and His Gospel." He shows a consistent conduct — his life confirms, and does not contradict, the Gospel. He practices constant cooperation — he shows an ability to get alongside all kinds of people, enjoying them, enlisting them, and engaging them for Christ's sake. And he exemplifies a conspicuous courage — his walk with God puts steel in his backbone.

A final word. The disciple-maker must seek to be steady and faithful in showing all of these marks. "Let us not be weary in well-doing, for in due season we shall reap, if we faint not" (Galatians 6:9). You will not object to a humorous conclusion to a very, very serious subject. A 104-year-old man was being interviewed by a newspaper reporter. "How did you do it?" the reporter asked. The centenarian answered, "I ate the right food, got plenty of sleep each night, didn't fool around, and never drank alcohol, smoked cigarettes, or chewed tobacco." The reporter said cynically, "I had an uncle like that but he died at fifty-five. How do you explain that?" The old man answered, "Oh, he just didn't keep it up long enough!" Are the five marks of the disciple-maker present and growing in your life?

Chapter 8

A Disciple-Maker's Desire for Unity

If there be therefore any consolation in Christ, if any comfort of love, if any fellowship of the Spirit, if any bowels and mercies, Fulfil ye my joy, that ye be like-minded, having the same love, being of one accord, of one mind. Let nothing be done through strife or vainglory; but in lowliness of mind, let each esteem other better than themselves. Look not every man on his own things, but every man also on the things of others. (Philippians 2:1-4)

Paul's letter to the Philippians was a very, very happy letter. Some form of the word "joy" occurs some nineteen times in the letter. Written by a man dragging a chain across the page as he wrote! Written from a Roman jail cell! Samuel Rutherford, the great Scottish Christian, once wrote from a prison cell, "Jesus Christ came into my cell last night, and every stone sparkled like a diamond and shone like a ruby." Paul's heart was full of the same experience of Jesus and the same elation over it.

However, there was a minor problem in the tone of the letter and in the fellowship of believers at Philippi. Epaphroditus had brought a report to Paul from Philippi to Rome, and the report glowed with praise — except for one "fly in the ointment." One element in the report brought by Epaphroditus caused Paul concern.

A certain undertone of disunity could be detected in the fellowship. The problem was apparently quite small, but it is never too soon to deal with a budding problem. A sign on a fruit market wall points out the infectious nature of some problems:

> *"That which today is only a spot,*
> *Tomorrow will be deadly rot."*

Problems in a Christian fellowship are like cancer in a human body. If neglected, they spread — and may kill. The secret of overcoming both cancer in the body and crisis in the fellowship is in early detection and rapid treatment.

Paul practiced both curative and preventive medicine in dealing with the problem. His tone is very tender. He does not rebuke or warn; he only exhorts. The situation in Philippi was very different from that at Corinth. He severely admonished and rebuked the Corinthians, even threatening to come to them "with a rod." But here, he writes with passion and gentleness. It must be noted, also, that he deals with the problem both positively (verses 1, 2) and negatively (verses 3, 4). He left no stone unturned in facing the problem and addressing his brothers and sisters about it.

The passage has a major theme and a minor theme. The major theme is that of Christian unity, and the minor theme is that of self-giving. They are "major" and "minor," not because of their respective significance, but because of the problem that is being dealt with. We will pursue the major theme in this study, the problem of Christian unity. The passage is absolutely packed with spiritual insight and wisdom, and needs to be "soaked in" by every Christian until its content and intent control his thought and life. Also, we must remember that we are looking at the content of the Philippian letter from the viewpoint of a disciple-maker. So I have called the study, "A Disciple-maker's Desire for Unity."

THE IDEAL OF CHRISTIAN UNITY

First, we must be aware of the *ideal of unity* among Christian believers. A casual reading of the New Testament will reveal how important this unity is. Indeed, in the great high priestly prayer of Jesus recorded in John 17, when Jesus reveals the intercession which He is practicing in Heaven throughout this age, he shows how crucial Christian unity is. "I pray that they all may be one; as thou, Father, art in me, and I in thee, that they also may be one in us: that the world may believe that thou has sent me....that they may be one, even as we are one: I in them, and thou in me, that they may be made perfect in one; and that the world may know that thou hast sent me" (John 17:21, 22, 23). So the unity of believers provides the "power base" to make the evangelistic and missionary thrust of the Gospel effective. J. O Frazer, the great missionary to China, once wrote, "Among Christian workers, true fellowship is as vital as evangelism." Indeed, true fellowship will always precede true evangelism. The power base for evangelism is absent if there is no rich, true fellowship among believers. Why is the desire for unity so important for a disciple-maker? What does this ideal entail?

First, unity among disciples will always involve *single-mindedness*. Jesus worked constantly to cement the Twelve together into a unit, a team. Near the very end, he was dealing with divisiveness among them, a divisiveness that had been stimulated by individual self-will among them. In our text, Paul pleads in these terms: "that ye be like-minded, ... of one mind" (verse 2). "Let this (a single, consolidated) mind be in you" (verse 5). Whereas James 1:8 speaks of "a double-minded man" (literally, "two-souled"), our text speaks of Christians being "single-minded" (literally, "one-souled"). Obviously, a group of "one-souled" or "single-minded" people is not common. However, the world is occasionally shocked when it sees the accomplishments of a few people who are welded together at the point of a white-hot commitment to a common cause. Any group of disciples can impact the world in an incredible way — if they are totally devoted to Christ and His Strategy, and if they are single-minded.

Second, unity among disciples will always involve *self-giving*. Another uncommon thing is a group of people who truly give themselves consistently and beyond the demands of a contract. True disciples don't wait for a job description or a paycheck before they give themselves away. However, any coach of team sports knows how deeply ingrained in each individual is the impulse of self-promotion and self-glory. Carl Sandburg once said, "Every human being has a secret desire to play Hamlet." Every human being wants to occupy center stage and be the key actor in the drama of life. Every human being wants to be "the greatest."

A little boy was strutting around his backyard, playing the hero in his own game of baseball. His baseball cap was in place on his head, and he had the ball in one hand and the bat in the other. He said to himself, "I'm the best hitter in the world." He threw the ball up into the air, swung the bat at it, and missed. "Strike one!" he shouted. He picked up the ball again, threw it into the air, swung again — and again missed. "Strike two!" he called out. He repeated the action, swinging the bat with all his might, and missing again. "Strike three!" he shouted, adding, "Wow! I'm the greatest *pitcher* in the world!"

Every human being has an almost incurable "self-curl" to his life, an inclination to favor and advance himself. This is a hangover from original sin, which is never really original, after all. Most people only think they are happy when they can survey their situation and sing,

*"Oh, what a beautiful morning! Oh, what a beautiful day!
I've got a beautiful feeling, Everything going my way!"*

Now, it is quite true that, if your goal is rosy feelings, you won't find them by exposing your hands and feet to the nails of a cross. But we must be very glad that Jesus did not pursue the goal of self-gratifying, rosy feelings. "He gave Himself for us," thank God! And we are to follow His example and give ourselves for others. Somewhere I found this great quote: "If we don't give out, we shall soon give out!" Jesus said, "Freely ye have received, freely give" (Matthew 10:8). Because of what we have received so bountifully from God's hand, we are exhorted, encouraged, and enabled to give to others. Go to the Dead Sea. Stand at the north end, and you will see that it has "freely received." But stand at the south end, and you will see why it is "Dead." It is all intake, with no corresponding output.

Verse 4 makes a strong appeal for self-giving when it says, "Look not every man on his own interests, but every man also on the interests of others." As Christians walk along the road of life, they will see people in all directions reaching out their hands for help of one kind or another. Each Christian can at least give something to those whose hands are nearest him. Trust God as your "booking agent" to bring you into touch with those He means you to reach. Every disciple-maker struggles to live toward other people, and he longs for his disciples to do the same.

During the summer of 1996, I took a group of 12 (Twelve!) disciples with me to Mindanao in the south Philippine Islands to teach several hundred Filipino pastors and Christian leaders. One morning, we had boarded the team bus to go to the teaching venue. One dear friend and fellow-disciple was seated beside me on the low luggage rack at the back of the bus. We were almost ready to pray as a team before departure. Suddenly, he leaned over to me and said, "Herb, I've never been around a bunch of men like this in my life. Just look at each one." As he spoke, he lifted an index finger and pointed one by one to the back of each man, saying softly as he pointed, "Selfless, selfless, selfless, selfless...." He will never know what spiritual satisfaction that brought to my heart.

Practically, how do we become self-giving individuals?

First, we must acknowledge the ideal of self-giving and make it a personal goal for ourselves. Second, we must cultivate the habit of noticing and paying attention to other people. The very term, "paying attention," suggests that there is a cost to the exercise—and there is! Third, we must learn to listen deeply and attentively to others. I read recently that the word for "listening" in one western Indian tribe is a word which means, "to spread out the ear." We must deliberately spread out our ears to others and let them fill them. Fourth, we must teach our egos to hold their breath (I borrowed that phrase, though I can't identify the source of it). Each of us is daily like an actor trying to impress an audience, and we love to occupy the center of the stage. Carl Sandburg was right when he said, "Every human being has a secret desire to play Hamlet." The hero may vary, but the desire and motive remain the same. But if you are to be a self-giving person, you must train your attention-hungry ego to stop striving for the spotlight and turn it on the other person. Fifth, we must empathize with the other person. "Empathy" is a compound word which means to "feel together." "Rejoice with those who rejoice, and weep with those who weep," the Bible says (Romans 12:15). Keep your "antennae" out, looking for someone who is happy about something today and let him know that you are happy about it, too. Share his celebration with him. Or find a person who is hurting (they are everywhere), and draw his pain into your heart. "If one part of the body (of Christ) suffers, all the other parts suffer with it; if one part is praised, all the other parts share its happiness"(I Cor. 12:26). Sixth, we must deliberately invest (the very word that is used several times in II Timothy) our lives in other people's lives. It was said of Oliver Goldsmith, the great author, that "he gave his life away in handfuls." With equally reckless abandonment, we must pour out our lives to others.

Many years ago, I saw this question: "What kind of church would my church be, if every other member were just like me?"

Apply the question in practical ways to your own personal experience. Apply it to your home: "What kind of home would my home be, if every other member were just like me?" Well, the chances are good that the others will be just like you — you will make them that way! Apply it to your workplace: "What kind of office would this office be, if every other worker were just like me?" Apply it to your nation: "What kind of country would this country be, if every other citizen were just like me?" Which would create a better church, a better disciple, a better home, a better office, a better community, a better nation, a better world — self-seeking or self-giving? Every disciple-maker longs for the self-giving of his disciples.

Third, unity among disciples will always involve *self-fulfilment*, both for the disciples and the disciple-maker. Every disciple-maker longs for his own true self-fulfilment. This may sound strange coming so closely on the heels of the previous point, but it is absolutely true. No person can be a true Christian or a true human being if he does not desire his own highest well-being, or his own truest and fullest self-fulfilment. Paul expressed it in our text in a beautiful phrase: "Fulfill ye my joy." It may be translated, "Fill up full my cup of joy." Paul had already expressed his great joy over their faith and love in Philippians 1:4, 9. Now he asks them to bring his joy to completion, to fullness. And he uses an aorist tense verb, indicating that they are to throw themselves into the act decisively and without reservation. They will find joy for themselves if they will live so unselfishly, and they will help Paul come to fullness of joy, also.

A mosaic of true Christian unity will be laced with single-mindedness, self-giving, and self-fulfilment. And a true disciple-maker will long for these threads in the tapestry of his own life and in the lives of his disciples.

THE INCENTIVES FOR CHRISTIAN UNITY

Our text clearly indicates some of the great *incentives* or motives for Christian unity. Verse one contains four "if" clauses, but actually it should be translated "since," or "in view of the fact." This is grammatically called a fulfilled condition. The four things mentioned are powerful facts in Christian experience, and provide four great motives for Christian unity. Do not hurry here. Take time to study Philippians 4:1 in numerous Bible translations. Use every tool of study you can find to aid you. This verse is a treasure hunt! Each phrase will require and repay close study.

Motive number one is the *consolation* that is found in Christ and His Gospel. The very experience of Christ's life that is common to all Christians is a massive stimulus to Christian fellowship and unity. "Since there is consolation in Christ" is the way this phrase has been translated. The word translated "consolation" (paraclesis) in the King James Version is a very expansive word. It may be translated, "exhortation," or "encouragement." "In view of the fact that there is a certain exhortation in Christ," Paul writes. But what does this phrase mean?

When a person has a genuine encounter with the saving Son of God, Jesus Christ, from the point of that encounter, that experience acts upon the believer's life like an "exhortation," or like a constraint, or like a spur. The Moffatt translation uses the word "stimulus." So the first motive for Christian unity is the experience of Christ's life. If the experience of Christ's life does not constrain you with heavy spiritual stimulation, it is doubtful that you are a Christian. Professions and pretensions of faith provide no motives to Christian action. Rules and rituals give no stimulus to Christian devotion. But when the pipeline of vital experience is opened between the sinner and the Savior, and the sinner is saved, then the trigger for motivation is in place. Does your soul find stimulus for Christian prayer, and praise, and practice in Christ Himself?

The *compulsion* of Christ's (Calvary) love is motive number two for Christian unity. This second motive is recorded in the phrase, "Since there is comfort (one translation says, 'an appeal') in love." I say it is "Calvary love" because the word is "agape," the word for self-disinterested, self-sacrificing love, God's distinctive kind of love. When a sinner is saved, "the love of God is shed abroad in his heart by the Holy Spirit who is given unto him" (Romans 5:5). "The love of Christ constrains us" (II Cor. 5:14). The love of Christ is like a great engine that pushes the Christian. When Divine love is born in the human soul at the new birth, there is a new pulse, a new impulse, a new force, a new driving power, in the individual's life. Love is a social concept, requiring at least two persons, a lover and a beloved, so when the love of Christ becomes operative in one's life, the person goes out from himself to meet his brother. Thus, Christian unity is born. Self-giving and Christian unity are Siamese twins in the Christian life.

The *communion* (koinonia) of the Holy Spirit is the third motive for Christian unity. This motive has several facets to it. "Since there is fellowship in the Spirit," Paul wrote. It is not certain whether this phrase means fellowship with the Holy Spirit, or fellowship with other brothers and sisters in the Holy Spirit, but they both are vitally true, and each provides a great motive for Christian unity. It is easy to see that a believer's fellowship with the Holy Spirit should provide a great stimulus for Christian unity. No man can "walk in the Spirit" (Galatians 5:16) and not be moved to live in fellowship with his fellow Christians. The "friend of God" will also be the "friend of sinners" and of saints. When believers are filled with the Spirit, they have a mutual magnet in them that adheres them to one another. Conversely, when they hold attitudes or display behavior that destroys the unity of the Church, they are despising the partnership of the Holy Spirit.

The fourth mentioned motive for Christian unity is Christ's *compassion*. "Since there are tender compassions and mercies," Paul says. Every Christian has experienced the super-abundance of Christ's compassion and mercy. The very mention of these should arouse celebration and worship in his heart. And he should live with compassion and mercy toward all men because he is aware of the importance of these factors in his own experience with God. Think of the impact on society that would be made if Christians overflowed with the same compassions and mercies toward others.

There is nothing more needed in the world today than widespread demonstrations of compassion by Christians. When you became a Christian, you became acutely aware of the compassion and mercy of God. You experienced the unbelievable forgiveness of God. Has God had compassion on us? Has God shown us mercy? Then surely we can demonstrate mercy and compassion toward other human beings. If you are constantly negative toward other people, critical, cynical, offended, resentful, you may need to go to Heaven's Mercy Seat for the first time. If you are a Christian and those attitudes persist, you need to quietly look on the Mercy Seat and see what great mercy has been given to you, and then begin to extend the same mercy to others.

These are the great incentives for Christian unity: the consolation there is in Christ, the compulsion there is in love, the communion of (in) the Holy Spirit, and the expression of Christ's compassion. With this kind of driving force, may we be unified as He wants us to be. A disciple-maker will grieve when he sees disunity among his disciples, and will rejoice when he sees that they are all tuned to the same chord.

THE INGREDIENTS OF UNITY

The text suggests three ingredients of Christian unity, and wisdom suggests several more. Let me mention them.

The first ingredient of unity suggested in the text is spiritual *humility*. In fact, one commentator said, "The theme of chapter two is how to maintain unity by humility." Verse three is a highwater verse of this paragraph. It contains both the negative and positive sides of humility. "Let nothing be done through strife or vainglory" is the negative side. These are surely carefully chosen words. "Strife" tears the other person down, while "vainglory" builds self up. The word for "strife" is translated "factiousness" elsewhere. The word "vainglory" means empty boasting, or selfish conceit. The world suffers from an excess of both of these problems. This is another symptom of man's sinful depravity. According to Galatians 5:20, competitive selfish ambition is a work of the flesh. This text calls it "empty glory." Somewhere I heard this adage: when wagons are moving down a street, it's the empty wagon that makes the most noise. Though any of us can be guilty of empty boasting at any time, it is actually both sad and stupid. Someone has said that it is like a balloon — the larger it stretches on the outside, the more the emptiness on the inside.

The sin of pride must be faced and dealt with by each Christian in ruthless realism and honesty. Augustine said, "It was pride that changed angels into devils, while it is humility that makes men like angels." Humility, the antidote for pride, is a strange virtue. When a Christian is conscious of humility, he just lost it! Spurgeon said, "Humility is to make a right estimate of one's self." It means seeing ourselves as we really are, and admitting to ourselves what we see. I'm not certain of the authorship of these words, but he was certainly trying to be objectively honest about his struggle with self and pride:

> *"Sometime when you're feeling important*
> *Sometime when your ego's way up,*
> *Sometime when you take it for granted*
> *That you are the prize-winning pup;*
> *Sometime when you feel that your absence*
> *Would leave an unfillable hole,*
> *Just follow these simple instructions*
> *And see how it humbles your soul.*
> *Take a bucket and fill it with water,*
> *Then put your hand in it up to your wrist,*
> *Now pull it out fast and the hole that remains*
> *Is the measure of how you'll be missed.*
> *You may splash all you please as you enter,*
> *And stir up the water galore,*
> *But stop and you'll find in a minute*
> *It's right back where it was before!"*

The positive side of humility is seen in the sentence, "But in lowliness of mind, let each esteem other better than themselves." The root Greek word translated "lowliness" is "tapeinos." If you look and listen carefully, you may be able to detect the beginning of an English word. This is the word from which we get our word, "tapestry." This verse calls for "tapestry-mindedness," or "carpet-mindedness" among Christians. They are to be willing to get down low among men without being threatened. A Christian should be so secure in Christ that he can allow others to step on him, and he will only pray that this will raise them closer to God! This is not timidity or "poor-spiritedness." Such a person is genuinely "poor in spirit." In such a spirit, the Christian is to "consider others better than himself." He may know assuredly that they are not better than himself, but he is to "consider" them so, and to proceed as if it were so. "In honor preferring one another," is the way Paul wrote it in Romans 12:10. What redemptive changes — of atmosphere, of attitudes, of actions, of results — would occur if Christians freely did this!

The second ingredient of unity suggested in the text is *spiritual harmony*. "Be like-minded, having the same love, being of one accord, of one spirit," says verse 2. "As though you had only one mind and one spirit among you," the Phillips paraphrase puts it, "cherishing a mutual love." The word translated "like-minded" is a strong word. It doesn't simply refer to a person's general thinking. It refers rather to the disposition and attitude of mind that is behind his general thinking. It refers to the mental paradigm or grid that determines all of his thinking. Only one paradigm should control the thinking of all Christians: "Let this mind be in you, which was also in Christ Jesus" (verse 5). The paradigm of Jesus was one of self-giving and service to others.

The word for mind in these text is *phronein*. In Romans 8:5, it is used for the flesh-dominated mind. This means that the entire mind of this kind of person operates from a fleshly or selfish perspective. In Romans 11:20, it is used for the lofty mind, or the person who is high-minded instead of humble. In Philippians 3:20 and Colossians 3:2, it is used for the earth-bound mind, or the mind of the person who is only interested in the things of this earth. In contrast to all of these mental control centers, all Christians are to learn more and more to think overwhelmingly like Jesus. His mind was a loving, serving, harmonious mind.

However, we must admit that this ideal must be attained; it cannot be taken for granted. Realistically, Christians may be divided into three distinguishable groups. The first group is made up of those who think "me." They always lead with the perpendicular pronoun, "I." The second group is made of those who think "us." They have a corporate consciousness, and see themselves as part of a unit. The third group consists of those who think "they." They think, speak, and act with other people in mind. The third group is the one Paul is calling for in our text.

All Christians should have such a walk with God and with other Christians that they are like keys tuned to the same chord and playing the same symphony. Every Christian must learn and relearn that Christianity is not a solo, it is a chorus. You cannot have harmony with just one note, there must also be other notes with which that note can blend. A facetious article appeared in a newspaper some years ago with the heading, "Bessie Smith Whistles Beethoven's Fifth Symphony." Nobody whistles a symphony, it takes an orchestra. Christianity requires a fellowship of believers, each giving up his autonomy and self-will to form a functional Body through which Christ reveals Himself. As a symphony, they will thus "sound together" in the society in which they exist.

The third ingredient of unity suggested in the text is spiritual *helpfulness*. If humility and harmony prevail among disciples, the reasonable outcome is that they will naturally find ways to help other people. They will "not look on their own interest, but each will look on the interests of others" (verse 4). The word "look" is the word from which we get out word, "scope." It suggests the adjusting of a lens, and it means to fix a gaze upon something so that purposes begin to form about that object. "Learn to see things from other people's point of view," the Phillips paraphrase says. This education requires a lifetime of learning, and we never graduate from this school. A Christian is to be so preoccupied with the interests of others that he forgets himself. What an ideal! Surely impossible without a miracle, but that is the glory of Christianity. A miracle-working God waits for a ready people.

This, then, is the Holy Spirit's great appeal for Christian unity. It is actually a call for maturity in thought, word and action. Unity is simply not possible without a humility that is bringing individuals every day into greater maturity in Christ. Of all people, a person who aspires to fulfill the Master's Great Commission by making disciples must desire those disciples to be in the closest fellowship both with Jesus and with other disciples.

E. Stanley Jones, the great missionary to India, told of a conversation he had one day with a conscientious Hindu. They were discussing religion and Jesus. Such a conversation in India usually gets around to the Cross of Christ, and this one followed the usual course. The Hindu asked Dr. Jones, "Don't you think atonement would mean attunement?" Then he added, "My life is like a set of sweet bells jangled out of tune by sin and evil, and I crave inward peace and harmony. To my mind, atonement would bring attunement to the nature of God — music instead of discord." A symphony, all instruments tuned to the same pitch, instead of a cacophony, a wild jangle of independent, self-tuned sounds! This is precisely the appeal of the Apostle in Philippians 2:1-4.

Let me conclude with an illustration from the life of the late great pastor, preacher, and radio teacher, Dr. J. Vernon McGee:

"When I first went to Nashville, Tennessee, as a pastor, some friends, thinking they were doing me a favor, called me and said, 'We have tickets for the Philadelphia Symphony Orchestra that is coming to town, and we want to take you as our guest.' Well, I love music, but I know nothing about it, and I can't sing — I always help congregational singing by keeping quiet. Frankly, I can't think of anything more boring than a whole evening of symphony! But they were so polite, and I wanted to be polite, so I accepted graciously and went along. I had never been to a thing like that before, and I was impressed by what I saw and heard.

We went in, took our seats, and in a few minutes the musicians began to drift in. They were in shirt sleeves for the most part, and each man went up to his instrument and started tuning it. The fellows with the fiddles too big to put under their chins sawed back and forth — oh, it sounded terrible. The fellows with the little ones put them under their chins and squeaked up and down on them. The ones with the horns — oh, my, nothing was in harmony. It was a medley of discordant, confused noise. Then after they got through with that kind of a disturbance, they all went out through the wings and disappeared. Another five minutes went by when all of a sudden the lights in the auditorium went off, the lights on the platform came on, and the musicians walked out. This time they had on their coats. My, they looked so nice. Each one came out and stood or sat at his instrument.

There was a hush in the auditorium, a spotlight was focused on the wings, and the conductor stepped out. When he did, there was thunderous applause for him. He bowed. Then he came up to the podium and picked up a thin little stick. He turned around again to the audience and bowed, then turned his back to the audience, lifted that little stick — total silence came over that auditorium. You could have heard a pin drop. Then he brought that little stick down. And goose bumps went all over me.

I never heard such music in all my life! Oh, what wonderful harmony there was! Today, we live in a wild world in which every man is tooting his own little tin horn. Everybody wants to tell you what he thinks. Everybody is playing his own little fiddle, and it is an absolute confusion of discord. Everything is out of tune. But one of these days the spotlight will go on, and the Lord Jesus Christ will come. When He comes back to this world, He is going to lift up His scepter, and everything that is out of tune will be corrected or removed. When He comes down with that scepter, what harmony will prevail! Meanwhile, I'm thankful today that I can bow my will to Him right here and right now. I can yield the little instrument of my life to Him. He told us that He will not break a bruised reed. He will fully restore it, put a new song in it, and give it a great place in His great choir. Then He will fill the universe with the songs of souls set free."

Chapter 9

From Throne to Throne by Way of the Earth

Let this mind be in you, which was also in Christ Jesus; Who, being in the form of God, thought it not robbery to be equal with God: But made himself of no reputation, and took upon him the form of a servant, and was made in the likeness of men; And being found in fashion as a man, he humbled himself, and became obedient unto death, even the death of the cross. Wherefore God also hath highly exalted him, and given him a name which is above every name: That at the name of Jesus every knee should bow, of things in heaven, and things in earth, and things under the earth; And that every tongue should confess that Jesus Christ is Lord, to the glory of God the Father. (Philippians 2:5-11; King James translation)

Keep on fostering the same disposition that Christ Jesus had. Though He was existing in the nature of God, He did not think His being on an equality with God a thing to be selfishly grasped, but He laid it aside, as He took on the nature of a slave and became like other men. Because He was recognized as a man, in reality as well as in outward form, He finally humiliated Himself in obedience so as to die, even to die on a cross. This is why God has highly exalted Him, and given Him the name that is above every other name, so that in the name of Jesus everyone should kneel, in heaven, on earth, and in the underworld, and everyone should confess that Jesus Christ is Lord, to the praise of God the Father. (Philippians 2:5-11; Williams translation)

Let Christ Jesus be your example as to what your attitude should be. For he, who had always been God by nature, did not cling to his prerogatives as God's equal, but stripped himself of all privilege by consenting to be a slave by nature and being born as mortal man. And, having become man, he humbled himself by living a life of utter obedience, to the extent of dying, and the death he died was the death of a common criminal. That is why God has now lifted him so high, and has given him the name beyond all names, so that at the name of Jesus every knee shall bow, whether in Heaven or earth or under the earth. And that is why, in the end, every tongue shall confess that Jesus Christ is the Lord, to the glory of God the Father. (Philippians 2:5-11; J. B. Phillips paraphrase)

Let your bearing towards one another arise out of your life in Christ Jesus. For the divine nature was his from the first; yet he did not think to snatch at equality with God, but made himself nothing, assuming the nature of a slave. Bearing the human likeness, revealed in human shape, he humbled himself, and in obedience accepted even death — death on a cross. Therefore God raised him to the heights and bestowed on him the name above all names, that at the name of Jesus every knee should bow — in heaven, on earth, and in the depths — and every tongue confess, 'Jesus Christ is Lord', to the glory of God the Father. (Philippians 2:5-11; New English Bible)

Let this same attitude and purpose and (humble) mind be in you which was in Christ Jesus. Let Him be your example in humility — Who, although being essentially one with God and in the form of God (possessing the fullness of the attributes which make God God), did not think this equality)with God was a thing to be eagerly grasped or retained; But stripped Himself (of all privileges and rightful dignity) so as to assume the guise of a servant (slave), in that He became like men and was born a human being. And after He had appeared in human form He abased and humbled Himself (still further) and carried His obedience to the extreme death, even the death of the cross! Therefore (because He stooped so low), God has highly exalted Him and has freely bestowed on Him the name that is above every *name, That in (at) the name of Jesus every knee should (must) bow, in heaven and on earth and under the earth, And every tongue (frankly and openly) confess and acknowledge that Jesus Christ is Lord, to the glory of God the Father. (Philippians 2:5-11; The Amplified Bible)*

The study of the doctrine of the Person of Christ is technically called "Christology." This great doctrinal passage from Paul's letter to the Philippians is nothing less than a systematic Christology. In fact, it is so full of great truths about Jesus Christ that it is easy to turn it into a mere study, and the heart fails to rise in praise to Jesus as it should before such a parade of truths. Every serious Christian should use this passage as a vehicle for adoration, pausing regularly in the passage to worship and adore the Person who is presented here. In this passage, we read of such breathtaking truths as the Preexistence of Jesus, the Incarnation of Jesus, the Humiliation of Jesus, the Crucifixion of Jesus, the Ascension of Jesus, and the Exaltation of Jesus. So it is indeed a systematic Christology! And the way these great truths are presented is even more remarkable. The passage contains a chain of mysterious and marvelous statements about Jesus, any one of which might make the subject for an entire volume of study. As a matter of fact, I have one volume of Christology in my personal library (A. B. Bruce's <u>The Humiliation of Christ</u>) which is essentially about one word (Jesus "stripped," or "emptied," Himself) in the text — and Bruce's large volume contains 447 pages! So the substance of eternity is contained in this paragraph of Scripture.

However, we must note the innocent setting in which such great truth is found. The church in Philippi had a small-scale problem of division in it. The tiny signs of a church split could be seen by a concerned observer. And Paul writes to nip this problem in the bud. In doing so, he incorporates into his statement the greatest paragraph on the Person of Christ ever written in human language. What is an incidental in the Philippian letter is the most fundamental of revelations about the Person of Christ. This is just like the Holy Spirit! How many times He hides fundamental realities in incidental occurrences, or sublime realities in simple settings. This passage spans the eternities; in fact, it could be called, "Jesus From Eternity to Eternity." It begins with Jesus in eternity past, follows the dizzying drop of His incarnation and humiliation, then attends Him in His Heavenly exaltation, which will continue forever. This passage will only be understood by the personal combination of an anointed mind and an adoring heart. Christ's redeeming activity has two great movements in it. First is His human emptying and second is His heavenly exaltation. Each of these two movements must be examined carefully.

HIS HUMAN EMPTYING

The first large movement in the text concerns the *human emptying of Christ*. We might study this humiliation of Jesus under four divisions which are revealed in verses six through eight. Each division contains a staggering truth about the condescension of Jesus.

Movement Number One: He who was totally God also became truly man. "Christ Jesus...being in the form of God, thought it not robbery to be equal with God: But made himself of no reputation, and took upon him the form of a servant, and was made in the likeness of men." "Being in the form of God, ... He was made in the likeness of men." Study carefully the various translations at the beginning of this study (and any more you may have). Compare the separate phrases in the different translations. We will need every possible shade of meaning in every word and phrase to see into these great truths. The Phillips paraphrase says that "Jesus had always been God by nature." The New English Bible says that "the divine nature was His from the first." The Williams paraphrase says, "He was existing in the nature of God." The Amplified Bible translates it: He was "essentially one with God, and in the form of God (possessing the fullness of the attributes which make God, God)."

At the very doorway of this great passage, we are confronted with the great fact of the preexistence of Jesus Christ. Jesus is a uniquely eternal Person! His life did not begin when He was conceived in the womb of the virgin Mary, or when He was born in Bethlehem. Oh, no! The word "being," or literally, "existing," clearly indicates that our Lord had a previous existence before Bethlehem. He Himself preceded and predated all the events of His own earthly life! The word used here for "being" occurs fifty-nine times in the New Testament and every time it has reference to prior existence. Prior to His birth at Bethlehem, Jesus the Son of God had existed for all eternity with God the Father and God the Holy Spirit. Jesus, with the Father and the Spirit, is everlastingly the living one.

Jesus Himself claimed preexistence. He often proclaimed His eternal existence to those around Him. In a classic passage in John six, He said that He "came down from heaven," and He indicates that He will return to where He was before. In another classic passage, He said, "Before Abraham was, I am" (John 8:58). The Jews understood His claim, because the text tells us that they immediately picked up stones with the intention of killing Jesus, for they recognized that He was implicitly identifying Himself as God, and they thought He was guilty of the "blasphemy" of making Himself equal with God. In John 17, the chapter which records the great High Priestly prayer of Jesus, verses five and seventeen refer directly to the eternal preexistence of Jesus. He asks the Father for the very glory which He had possessed with the Father "before the world was."

Jesus' claim of preexistence agrees perfectly with all of the writers of the New Testament. Consider briefly the testimony of the Apostle John. In John 1:1-2, he used a verb ("was") which indicates that Jesus always was, and that there was never a time when He was not. Consider, too, the testimony of the Apostle Paul. In II Corinthians 8:9, he wrote, "For ye know the grace of our Lord Jesus Christ, that, though he was rich, yet for your sakes he became poor, that ye through his poverty might be rich." Jesus could only have been "rich" in Heaven before coming to the earth and becoming a man. Therefore, He existed prior to coming to this world. Furthermore, we can see the nature of Christ's incarnation in this verse. When a rich man becomes poor, his mode of existence has changed, but not his nature as a human being. When Jesus became "poor" in His incarnation, His mode of existence changed, but not

His nature as God. Then, in Colossians 1:17, Paul said, "He (Jesus) is before all things, and by Him all things consist." The preposition that is used denotes that which is prior in time to all other things. All created things had a point of origin, but Christ did not. In fact, the Bible tells us that "all things were created by Him (Jesus)." The One through whom everything was called into existence necessarily existed before all else was created. Just as the artist existed before the portrait that he painted, and the architect existed before the building that he designed, so God the Son existed before the universe that He brought into being. The writers of the New Testament unanimously agree about the preincarnate existence and glory of Jesus Christ.

But this passage tells us much more. It not only reveals the fact of His preexistence; it also points out the form of it. "Christ Jesus, existing in the form of God." "Existing in the nature of God," the Williams translation says. "Being essentially one with God (possessing the fullness of the attributes which make God God)," the Amplified Bible puts it. "He had always been God by nature," the Phillips paraphrase translates it. The word translated "form" in the King James translation does not refer to a physical or outward form or shape. God is Spirit (John 4:24), and does not innately possess outward form or shape. The word "form" in our text means "essence" or "reality." Jesus was throughout eternity past in the "essence" or "reality" or "nature" of God. To say that Jesus was "existing in the nature of God" is the highest possible claim that He is totally God, or as the old creed says, "He is very God of very God." Jesus is Himself absolute Deity, a co-participant with God the Father and God the Holy Spirit in that Divine essence which constitutes God, God. So Jesus Christ is perfectly identified here with the being, nature, and personality of God — Himself being God!

While the great astronomer, Johan Kepler, was observing the stars one night, he explained his activity with these words: "I am thinking God's first thoughts after Him." But the thoughts expressed in our text predate the stars! Here, we are thinking over again the first thoughts of God. Here the vastness of eternity unfolds before us.

Now we come to the "dizzying drop" which I referred to earlier. He who was totally God became truly man. Again, Phillips translates it, "He who had always been God by nature, did not cling to His rights as God's equal." "He did not snatch at his rights," another translation says. We are great "snatchers" of rights and advantages — just look at the daily newspapers! "He did not regard His equality with God a thing to be seized upon." The word means to "clutch," or "cling," or "hoard.' Jesus was so absolutely sure of His Godhood — of His total equality with God as God -- that He did not have to hoard it. He could freely give up His rights, advantages, and powers, knowing that no loss could permanently threaten Him. Here was the contest of redemption. The first Adam made a frantic attempt to seize equality with God (Genesis 3:5); but Jesus, the last Adam, being sure of Godhood, voluntarily gave up His Divine rights and advantages.

"And He was made in the likeness of men." Let these words reach the deep of your person: God became man! The word "likeness" means similarity but with a difference. Jesus became a man, similar to each of us — but with a difference! Though He was genuinely human, He was unique among humans in that He was without sin. The New Testament writers use an impressive array of words and phrases to present the incarnation ("in-fleshment") of God in Christ. John 1:14 says that He "became flesh." Galatians 4:4 says that he was "born of a woman." Romans 1:3 says that "He was born of the seed of David according to the flesh." I Timothy 3:16 declares that "God was manifested in the flesh." Hebrews 2:14 indicates that "He became a partaker of flesh and blood." And His time on earth is referred to as "the days of His flesh" (Hebrews 5:7).

We must never allow the incarnation of Christ to fade in our minds or hearts. "Jesus" is the human name of God! And we must not confuse this truth. The incarnation is not the deifying of man; it is the humanizing of God. It is not man rising into Godhood; it is God condescending into manhood. In His incarnation, He was as perfectly united with man as He had always been -- and remained -- perfectly united with God. This incredible fact brings many previously impossible things into the human situation. For example, when God became man in the incarnation of Christ, for the first time in His eternal existence, God's nature had substance. And for the first time in His eternal existence, God now had a nature that was capable of dying! So the stage is now set for a transaction of eternal redemption to be made. God is on earth as a man, with a mortal human nature — something awfully big is in the making! The vital ingredients of a coming Calvary are now in place.

C. S. Lewis, the British scholar and Christian, wrote these helpful words:

"Did you ever think, when you were a child, what fun it would be if your toys could come to life? Well, suppose you could really have brought them to life. Imagine turning a tin soldier into a real little man. It would involve turning the tin into flesh. And suppose the tin soldier did not like it. He is not interested in flesh; all he sees is that the tin is being spoilt. He thinks you are killing him. He will do everything he can to prevent you. He will not be made into a man if he can help it. What you would have done about that tin soldier I do not know. But what God did about us was this. The Second Person in God, the Son, became human Himself; was born into the world as an actual man — a real man of a particular height, with hair of a particular color, speaking a particular language, weighing so many pounds. The Eternal Being, who knows everything and who created the whole universe, became not only a man but a babe, and before that a fetus inside a woman's body. If you want to get the hang of it, think how you would like to become a snail or a crab."

Think of it! The great Creator has become a creature in His own creation — in order to recreate both the sin-tainted creation and the sin-infected creature, man. The glorious Son of God voluntarily forsook the splendor of His pre-existent state in Heaven and became as genuinely human as we ourselves are — and all for our sake.

Some years ago, I read with great pleasure Ernest Gordon's partial autobiography entitled <u>Miracle On the River Kwai.</u> Gordon was a British Highland soldier captured by the Japanese during World War II. He was kept in a POW camp in a Burmese jungle. The prisoners of war were forced to build a railroad for the Japanese in the jungle. Gordon nearly starved along with the other prisoners, and became the victim of numerous tropical diseases. He was not a Christian when he was placed in the death house and left to die. However, a fellow prisoner took Gordon out, shared his meager food rations with him, and nursed him back to health. This friend also introduced Gordon to Christ. The story is the remarkable story of faith's triumph over the many obstacles that stood against it, or the story of Christ's triumph among His helpless people. Years later, when Ernest Gordon was chaplain at Princeton University, he wrote that Jesus Christ "came into our Death House, to lead us out and deliver us to full spiritual health." But before He could come "into our Death House," He first had to become a man. When Jesus came to the earth, He might have said, "I am what I was — God. I was not what I am — man. I am now both — God and man." The Son of God became also the Son of Man. He who was totally God became truly man.

Movement Number Two: He who was the Greatest Somebody in the universe became the least nobody in the universe. The King James Version explains it by saying, "He made Himself of no reputation," and "He humbled Himself." The Amplified Bible says, "He stripped Himself (of all privileges and rightful dignity)." The Williams translation says, "He laid it aside," and "He humiliated Himself." The New English Bible says, "He made Himself nothing." Jesus Himself said that He was "set at nought" (Mark 9:12). All of these statements are attempts to explain one of the biggest words in the Bible. The root word is "kenosis," and refers to the self-emptying of Jesus in coming to the earth. But what did Jesus strip from Himself, or empty Himself of, in coming to the earth? P. T. Forsyth used an extraordinary term for it; he called it Christ's "self-disglorification." What did Jesus strip Himself of in Heaven before coming to this earth? This is a delicate and difficult question, and requires suitable thought and effort to answer.

John Milton, one of the greatest of Christian poets, wrote:

> *"That glorious Form, that Light insufferable*
> *He laid aside: and here with us to be,*
> *Forsook the courts of everlasting day,*
> *And chose with us a darksome house of mortal clay."*

But just exactly what did Jesus "lay aside" in Heaven? Did He lay aside His Godhood, His Deity, His Divine Nature? Certainly not! Indeed, He could not lay aside His very "nature." He was just as much God when He walked the streets of Nazareth as when He trod the courts of Heaven. Did He strip Himself of His sinlessness? Certainly not! He was just as surely sinless and perfectly pure on earth as He had always been from eternity. He was as sinless and holy while on earth as a man as He had been when He was only God and in Heaven. He stripped Himself of the outward expression of His Deity, of the outward manifestation of His Heavenly glory. Be very careful here. Jesus stripped Himself only of the expression of His Deity; He did not give up the possession of His Deity. He was always fully God, even when His Godhood was veiled in human flesh. He stripped Himself of the independent use of His Divine rights and powers. He laid aside the glory, privileges and majesty that had always been His.

Notice the emphasis in all of these phrases on the voluntary nature of Christ's actions. He was coerced only by His love for us. "He made Himself of no reputation." "He took upon Him the form of a servant." "He humbled Himself." "He stripped Himself." "He became obedient unto death."

There is an incredible illustration of all of the movements of this text in the great foot-washing episode in John thirteen. In that story, Jesus did seven things, and those seven things reveal "Jesus From Eternity to Eternity." Each of them has an exact counterpart in our text. Read John 13: 1-13, and note the seven actions of Jesus: (1) He stood up; (2) He put something off; (3) He put something on; (4) He poured something out; (5) He washed His followers with that which He poured out — and "wiped them with the towel," suggesting a finished work; (6) He returned to His original position and reassumed His original garments; and (7) He sat down again. Can anyone miss that sequence? This is the eternal history of Jesus. One awful but glorious day in Heaven, He stood up — and prepared to go to Bethlehem and Calvary . . . .

Many people will remember the English Duke of Windsor as the man who was at one time the King of England, but who abdicated his throne and stripped himself of the royal vesture of his rightful office in order to marry Wallace Simpson, the woman he loved. Even so, Jesus abandoned the eternal throne of Heaven that was His by right, in order to fully identify Himself with you and me, whom He loved. For a moment, return to the human illustration I have just shared, and put yourself "into the shoes" of the lady in the story. When Mrs. Simpson was on the point of marrying the King of England, the newspapers at home and abroad had some very unkind things to say about her. They told the world how she had already wrecked two marriages. They indicated that she would marry the King whether she loved him or not, for his position and his wealth. All in all, they made her out a rather cheap woman. We will probably never know just what her reactions were to all this. But if she was a sensitive woman, she must have agonized over the reactions. But even if she felt unspeakably unworthy, she could have said something like this: "The King of the greatest empire on earth has loved me enough to uncrown himself for me." Christian, the King of Heaven has loved you enough to uncrown Himself for you. What should your response be, personally and practically?

But there is still more that must be said before we leave this movement. Not only did He leave the throne and lay aside His glory; it wasn't even known by most people where He walked that He had ever occupied a throne or had possessed any glory. "He was in the world, and the world was made by Him, but the world knew Him not" (John 1:10). He Himself once said, "There is one among you whom ye know not." He not only was God incarnate; He was also God incognito.

John D. Rockefeller, Jr., used to walk around Rockefeller Center when the skyscraper was in the process of construction. He would stand on the sidewalk and watch the advancing construction for a few minutes every day. One day, a watchman accosted him. "Move along, buddy," he growled. "You can't stand loafing here." He quietly withdrew, unrecognized. Jesus often told people whom He helped to "tell no one." Most people would have accelerated their publicity machine into high gear, but Jesus was content to be an unknown.

Suppose that a general of the United States Army walked into the soldiers' common barracks. The moment he enters, the men snap to attention and salute, because they recognize the uniform and the insignia of his rank. They continue at attention until he says, "At ease." If he sits down to talk with them, their restraint is obvious. He is a general, they are enlisted men, and they are conscious of the difference in rank and position. However, if he should enter the barracks without the emblems of his rank and incognito, there would be quite a different atmosphere. The men would take him to be one of themselves, would talk more freely with him, and might be flippantly familiar with him. Even so, when Jesus "made Himself of no reputation," He merely took off His insignia. His rank had not changed, though the outward signs of it were somewhat hidden. The people who were near Him received Him as a man. Furthermore, He put Himself at the mercy of friends and enemies alike.

I spent five years of my life in Fort Worth, Texas, where I attended seminary. The name of Dutch Meyer was a familiar name in the Fort Worth area. Dutch Meyer was the longtime, legendary, revered former Texas Christian University football coach. The Daniel-Meyer Coliseum on the TCU campus was named for him. One day some years ago an older gentleman dressed in old, rumpled clothes came into the coliseum offices with an armload of newspapers. He placed the papers on the floor, said, "Here are some newspapers," and started toward the door. The secretary stopped him. When she questioned him he said that he had read in the newspaper that they were collecting used newspapers and that he had brought some in. The secretary told him to remove the papers; he couldn't leave them there. But this idea did not appeal to the old gentleman. When the young TCU athletic director came out to see the cause of the disturbance, he, too, suggested that the man remove the papers. When he refused, they asked him to leave the office. He refused to do that, too. Then the athletic director went to the phone and called campus security requesting that this man be removed from the office. When the veteran campus security officer arrived and was told the situation, he said to the younger office staff, "I beg you to reconsider your request. This man is Dutch Meyer. You're about to have him thrown out of his own building!" "Jesus was in the world, and the world was made by Him, and the world knew Him not. He came unto His own (world), and His own (people) received Him not." A blind and arrogant world threw the Son of God out of His own building, and He hardly defended or explained Himself! He was far greater than a five-star general in Heaven, but He came to earth without His insignia showing. The Greatest Somebody in the universe became the least nobody in the universe — voluntarily.

Movement Number Three: He who was Master of all became the slave of all. "He took upon Him the form of a servant" (verse 7). "I am among you as he who serves," Jesus said. He who was eternally and rightfully accustomed to giving orders voluntarily placed himself in the subordinate position of taking orders. The word "form" in verse seven is the same word that is used in verse six. The same Jesus that was in His very nature and essence, God, took on the nature and essence of a slave. He submitted Himself to authentic servanthood, always considering others before Himself (verse 4). In fact, He declared that this was one of the primary reasons for His coming: "The Son of Man did not come to be served, but to serve, and to give His life a ransom for many" (Matthew 20:28). Remember that a slave has no rights of his own, no will of his own, no property of his own, and no schedule of his own. During his teenage years, He served as an apprentice carpenter to his foster father, Joseph. He is now making yokes for cattle, but before He came, He was making worlds. It is simply part of the "incarnational package" that the Lord of the universe became a lowly servant among men.

Movement Number Four: He who was Life DIED! The text says that Jesus "emptied Himself," and this speaks of His incarnation. Then it says that He "humbled Himself," and this speaks of His crucifixion. So His voluntary condescension was in two successive stages: first, to the earth, and then on the earth. The first stage was a humiliation *to* humanity, and the second was a humiliation *in* humanity. He "became obedient unto death — even the death of the Cross!" "He went even to the extent of dying, and the death that He died was the death of a common criminal" (Phillips). "He carried His obedience to the extreme death, even the death of the cross" (Amplified). Note carefully the giant word, "obedience," and remember that Jesus' obedience to His Father was total and perfect. "I do always those things that please Him," He declared. "One man's disobedience" had to be undone "by the obedience of One" (Romans 5:19). Adam's obedience would have been unto life, but instead, he disobeyed — unto death. So Jesus, the last Adam, must now obey unto death, that His obedience unto death might bring life unto us, the disobedient ones. What a Gospel!

During some turbulent days in ancient Rome, a slave heard that his master's name was on the death list. He quickly put on his master's cloak and quietly awaited the arrival of the political killers. When they found the slave dressed in his master's clothing, they killed him, supposing him to be the master. In the same manner, the Master of the universe, the Lord Jesus Christ, took on Himself the cloak of our humanity — and died. The death He endured was the death we deserved.

The kind of death Jesus died — the death of the cross — was the very symbol of disgrace, agony, and shame. And the reality was far, far worse than the mere symbol! When Paul said, "even the death of the cross," you can feel Paul recoiling from this terrible thought. You see, the mere death of Christ was not enough. If His death was all that was called for, then He could have been killed by

Herod while yet in His infancy and the world would have been saved. The death of Jesus acquires its redemptive quality from two things: (l) The life of perfect obedience which lay behind it, and (2) The kind of death it was -- "even the death of the cross." It is amazing that Jesus could die. It is more amazing that He would die. It is more amazing yet that He should die. It is still more amazing that He did die. But the most amazing thing of all is that He died "even the death of the cross!" As if crucifixion were not terrible enough in itself, to compound both the horror and the amazement, the law of Moses attached a curse to anyone who suffered this mode of death (Deuteronomy 21:23). But again, wonder of wonders, our loving Father turned this around to make a Gospel out of it. *"Christ hath redeemed us from the curse of the law, being made a curse for us" (Galatians 3:13).* Everything the world and the devil means to be evil to us, God turns it into good! Hallelujah! And Paul uses all of this to appeal for our humility and unity!

> *When I survey the wondrous cross,*
> *On which the Prince of Glory died,*
> *My richest gain I count but loss,*
> *And pour contempt on all my pride."*

Gladys Aylward, the missionary to China, about whose life the Hollywood film, "The Inn of the Sixth Happiness," was made, said in an address to Christian college students, "Are you thinking of going to the mission field for thrilling and romantic experiences? If so, don't come! They aren't there. Instead, it is following Jesus, step by step, from the graveyard of selfish ambitions into the life of God." But this is not only the standard for a missionary. It is the daily standard for every Christian. The Christian life is following Jesus, step by step, from the graveyard of selfish ambitions into the life of God.

HIS HEAVENLY EXALTATION

The second large movement in the text concerns the *heavenly exaltation of Christ* after His human emptying and humiliation. This passage is equally as great in pointing out the exaltation of Jesus as it is in pointing out the humiliation of Jesus. Note the dimensions of His exaltation.

First, it is a *deserved* exaltation. This is indicated by the word, "wherefore." The exaltation of Christ follows reasonably and inevitably on the heels of His humiliation. The masculine pronoun "him" is used twice in verse nine, and the human name, "Jesus" is used in verse ten. So the person who is exalted in verses nine through eleven is the same person who "emptied Himself" and "humbled Himself" in the preceding verses. In the Greek text, the word "Himself" in all these phrases comes before the verb, emphasizing that the self-emptying was of Christ's own free will. It was a totally voluntary act. At the beginning of the redeeming process He stripped Himself in Heaven of the insignia of royalty, glory, majesty, and honor, and came into humanity by a miraculous supernatural act. At the end of the redeeming process He humbled Himself and gave Himself up to die.

Give much thought to these next sentences. It was not because of His essential glory as the Eternal Christ that He was recrowned with supernal glory. No! The exaltation declared in Philippians 2:9-11 is given in exact proportion to His voluntary humiliation. How deep was His humiliation? You may answer that question by measuring the height of His exaltation. How high is His exaltation? You may answer that question by placing a measuring line alongside His humiliation as presented in Philippians 2:6-8. His ascent to the throne of glory was only His descent reversed. His "up-rising" in verses nine through eleven is an outcome of His "down-stooping" and "down-stepping" in verses six through eight. Considering His Divine Personhood, any exaltation that followed these acts of self-giving was certainly a deserved exaltation. The exaltation corresponds to the humiliation. The exaltation was not arbitrary, but reasonable. The outcome did not depend on the thoughtless whim of a Divine dictator, but on the reasonable heart of a Heavenly Father. The reasons for His exaltation may be seen by studying the Epistles of the New Testament. For example, in Hebrews, it is His Personal superiority that merits His exaltation. In Colossians, it is

His Personal supremacy in creation (both the old material creation, and the new spiritual creation, the Church) that merits His exaltation. In our text in Philippians, it is His Personal sufficiency in self-emptying and redemption that merits His exaltation. So His exaltation is fully deserved.

Second, His exaltation was a *divine* exaltation. "Wherefore God hath also highly exalted Him." Do you see the contrast: Jesus humbled Himself, but God exalted Him. This is a law in the realm of grace: "He that exalteth himself shall be humbled, but he that humbleth himself shall be exalted." Note that the initiative in this exaltation belongs solely and exclusively to God. It is a rule that God initiates only what He appreciates. God acts within the limits of His own approval. God sets the standard for His own actions. No other cause except the pleasure of God would ever draw the approval of God. God exalted Jesus because it was perfectly suitable to His nature to do so.

Third, it was a *defined* exaltation. We are left in no doubt about the degree or kind of this exaltation. "God has highly exalted Him, and given Him a name which is above every name." The verb, "highly exalted," is used only in this one instance, and is here applied only to Jesus. It literally means that "God has super-exalted Him," or that God has elevated Him in a transcendentally glorious manner. The word that is used indicates double-barreled exaltation. It would help us to appreciate this statement if we brought in a great supportive passage from Paul's exalted letter to the Ephesians. Ephesians 1:19-23, where Paul speaks of "the exceeding greatness of God's power toward us who believe, according to the working of His mighty power, Which He wrought in Christ, when He raised Him from the dead, and set Him at His own right hand in the heavenly places, Far above all principality, and power, and might, and dominion, and every name that is named, not only in this world, but also in that which is to come: And hath put all things under His feet, and gave Him to be the head over all things to the church, Which is His body, the fulness of Him that filleth all in all."

Furthermore, God has "given Him a name which is above every name." Remember that this bestowal follows His self-emptying. In His humiliation, He was given the name "Jesus," so it is likely that the name given Him in His exaltation is the name, "Lord."

Fourth, it is a *demanding* exaltation. "At the name of Jesus every knee should bow, of things in heaven, and things in earth, and things under the earth; And that every tongue should confess that Jesus Christ is Lord, to the glory of God the Father." One day there is going to take place a universal acknowledgment of the Lordship of Christ over all creation and over every created intelligence. There will be no exemption, no exception, and no exclusion. That day will be marked by a conscious reversal of man's previous judgment about Jesus. When he was on earth, man said, "He is worthy of death, even the death of the Cross." But now, God speaks, and tells us the total, unconditional, undeniable and undebatable truth about Jesus. How shocking that day will be to human beings who tragically over-estimated their ability to evaluate such a Person as Jesus!

One of Hans Christian Anderson's fairy tales tells of an emperor who wanted to see how his people behaved in his absence. So he dressed as a beggar and visited the city. The people promptly threw him out! A few days later, when he came in triumph in his golden carriage, everybody bowed low as it passed. However, when they looked into the carriage to see the emperor, they were astonished to see the face of the very beggar they had treated so badly. While they thought he was a beggar, and treated him as such, he was actually the Emperor of the Realm!

Two thousand years ago, the Emperor of the Realm disrobed Himself in His throne room of His royal robes and dressed Himself in the lowly garb of our frail and poor humanity. He came to this earth and lived as a man among men. Man's rejection of Him was shocking, and it has continued for two thousand years. He has been "despised and rejected of men" for a long, long time now. They have glibly and impudently rejected Him without investigation or consideration, without intelligence or integrity, declaring Him to be a "mere man," or merely a "good man," one who has no claim on their lives or their allegiance. But like the citizens in the fairy story, they will see and acknowledge that the "beggar" is in fact the Emperor of the Realm. They will recognize and declare with tongue and knee that the man of Galilee is the King of Kings and Lords of Lords.

This acknowledgment of Jesus will involve universal worship. "Every knee will bow" before Christ. Every knee — the proud Pharisee's knee, the arrogant rebel's knee, the atheist's knee, the cynic's knee, the stubborn and unbent knee, my knee and yours — shall bow before Christ. And it will involve universal witness. *"And every tongue shall confess that Jesus Christ is Lord, to the glory of God the Father."* Every tongue — the idler's tongue, the pagan's tongue, the heathen's tongue, the unbeliever's tongue, the gossiping tongue, the boasting tongue, the cursing tongue, the criticizing tongue, the blaspheming tongue, etc. — these will suddenly be transformed into confessing tongues! The sinner's tongue that always disagreed with God when the subject was Jesus, will now totally agree with God's full assessment of His Son. And the saint's tongue, which has already humbly agreed with God about Jesus in order to be saved (Romans 10:9-10), will now happily agree with God about Jesus in this great universal acknowledgment of His Lordship.

Let these words come home to your heart, dear Christian. Let them bring both conviction and invitation to you. How bent is your knee to Christ — on His terms — today? How loose is your tongue in confessing Him among men? Is the bending of your knee merely a polite and convenient courtesy? Is the use of your tongue for Him a mere stammer instead of a clear and uncompromising statement? Before you answer too quickly, be sure that you reexamine His terms as they are stated in Philippians 2:3-4.

HIS HOLY EXAMPLE

The third thing to see in this great passage is the *holy example of Christ*. Before we leave this glorious text, let's remind ourselves of the setting, or the context, of this passage. We must remember the background of these great words. The passage is used to encourage us to follow the holy example of Jesus in emptying Himself. Read verses three and four again. "Let nothing be done through strife or vainglory; but in lowliness of mind let each esteem other better than themselves. Look not every man on his own things, but every man also on the things of others." Verses three and four provide the subject, and verses five through eleven should give us our education. What is the highest ideal of human character? Is it (as the world thinks) human power, clout, and macho muscle? Is it intellectual prowess, such as that of the scientist or philosopher? Is it wealth and riches? "I went into the sanctuary of God; then I understood" (Psalm 73:17). The answer is to be found in the heart of God. It is reflected in His Word in such passages as our text.

Here is Heaven's supreme conception of character. This is what eternity enthrones. The nature that stoops, cares, loves, forgives, and saves others; this is the ideal type. In order to see this, we must attend the School of Calvary and see Jesus modeling the ultimate lesson. Our education as Christians begins and ends at Calvary. What do we learn at the cross? At the cross, we receive the explanation for Jesus' self-emptying. You see, it is tragically easy to think that humility is the end in itself. We think, "If I can just achieve and maintain humility, I would reach the ultimate goal of being a Christian." But read the text carefully. "Jesus humbled Himself." For what purpose? To become obedient. To what end? "Obedient unto death, even the death of the cross." And for what purpose did He die that death? To save others! The object of all of His redeeming activity was others. The ideal Christian character is reached when a Christian lives for others and their highest welfare — on Christ's terms.

We find the Supreme Example of this ultimate lesson in the Person and history of Jesus. These verses comprise a fabulous Christology, but they are presented to give an example of how important it is to live and die for others. While everybody else is living for "vainglory" (verse 3), Jesus laid aside true glory, the glory He had had with the Father "before the world was." To save others!

If we have our wits about us at all, we will see that we are only truly Christian when we humble ourselves and pour out our lives to save and build others — like Jesus did. But now another problem arises. How can we be expected to imitate His act of self-renunciation and ministry to others. Who are we? What glory do we have to lay aside? None at all, nothing but empty vain-glory, only a thing of sin and shame. Yet, each of us may "have the same mind;" each of us may let the mind of Christ be in us, that mind which led Him to leave "His own things" for the sake of "the things of others."

Take a final look at Jesus. While He was revealing the ultimate extreme of self-giving, His enemies unwittingly gave Him the greatest compliment ever paid Him. They said, "He saved others; Himself He cannot save" (Mark 15:31; Matthew 27:42). They were better theologians than they knew. Their words reveal the master principle of human redemption and the master lesson of Christian discipleship. If I am to be used of God, I cannot save myself. "He who would save His life shall lose it, but whoso would lose His life for My sake and the Gospel's, shall save it." If Christ had saved Himself from the Cross, He could not have saved us from sin. To save us, Himself He could not save.

"He saved others." He didn't save money, He didn't save His own skin, He saved others. This is a message that should produce delight in the hearts of sinners. All sinners need to be saved, and if Jesus saved others, then why shouldn't He save me? This is a message that should stimulate dedication in the hearts of saints. I should be doing the same thing that Jesus did, giving my life for the sake of others. But tragically, this is a message that will produce final despair in the hearts of some. He save others, but He didn't save me! If His enemies had only realized it, even as they were sarcastically admitting that He had saved others, His very dying at that moment was to save them! But those hard-hearted men, by their own use of that word, "others," placed themselves outside the reach of His saving grace. When they said, "He saved others," they were necessarily saying, "He has not saved us." By that word, "others," they excluded themselves. And it is still true that the only ones who are excluded from His salvation are the ones who are self-excluded. The only ones who cannot be saved are those who will not be saved.

"Others, Lord, yes, others, Let this my motto be,
And as I live for others, Let me live for Thee."

Chapter 10

Does Obedience Produce Slavery or Freedom?

Wherefore, my beloved, as ye have always obeyed, not as in my presence only, but now much more in my absence, work out your own salvation with fear and trembling. For it is God which worketh in you both to will and to do of his good pleasure. Do all things without murmurings and disputings: That ye may be blameless and harmless, the sons of God, without rebuke, in the midst of a crooked and perverse nation, among whom ye shine as lights in the world; Holding forth the word of life; that I may rejoice in the day of Christ, that I have not run in vain, neither laboured in vain. Yea, and if I be offered upon the sacrifice and service of your faith, I joy, and rejoice with you all. For the same cause also do ye joy, and rejoice with me. (Philippians 2:12-18)

The second chapter of Philippians has two themes — a large, major theme and a small, "minor" theme. The major theme of the chapter is humility. Indeed, this is without question the greatest chapter in the Bible on the subject of humility. The master-key of this chapter, and the master-key of Christianity, is humility. The "minor" theme of the chapter is obedience. Our text is an example of the importance of obedience.

Modern man, captured by secular humanism, has raised his voice in loud protest against the virtues of humility and obedience.

He cries, "Humility is an unnecessary cowering and groveling before a supposed God — because of a superstitious fear of the unknown. And obedience is nothing short of slavery." He taunts the Christian with the words, "Where is this 'freedom in Christ' we hear so much about, if we must obey Him?"

The brilliant poet Shelley spoke for such men in one of his poems:

"Power, like a desolating pestilence,
Pollutes whatever it touches; and obedience,
The bane of all genius, virtue, freedom, truth,
Makes slaves of men, and of the human frame
A mechanized automaton."

"Obedience makes slaves of men," said Shelley, and his complaint may be valid in some cases. As examples: (1) There is extreme peril in full obedience to any mere mortal man. Such unquestioning obedience may easily become slavery. (2) There is grave peril also in full obedience to any church or religious system (indeed, to any system of any kind). I was astounded to read Ignatius Loyola's statement in the Constitution of the Catholic Jesuit order: "We must, if anything appears to our eyes, white, which the Church declares to be black, also declare it to be black." This is dangerous, debilitating, and likely damning, obedience to a church and a religious system. This makes religious slaves of men, and the most binding, demanding, and destructive kind of slavery is religious slavery.

The Christian's obedience is to be only to the Lord! And yet, we must make the practical acknowledgment that we will likely render obedience to Him only if we first hear His truth through His church. When Christ's minister speaks to us the Word of the Lord, and we obey it, we are obeying Christ. So the Christian's powers of discrimination and discernment must be developed (Hebrews 5:14) so he can detect the difference between the Word of God and the mere words of men. Again, disciple-making is a paramount necessity for this development. Jesus said, "If any man will do His will, he shall know of the doctrine, whether it comes from God or some other source." If any Christian sincerely wants to hear the Word of God that he may earnestly obey it, he will hear it — with understanding.

No Christian dares to obey any man purely passively and unthinkingly, lest Shelley's charge becomes true and that Christian becomes "a mechanized automaton." But the obedience to Jesus Christ rendered by a Spirit-filled Christian is not liable to this error. We can trust Jesus Christ as we can trust no mere mortal man. For one thing, His guidance is perfect, and for another, He only seeks our highest good.

Having said all of that, it must also be stated that it is a badge of honor and freedom in the New Testament for a Christian to call himself "a bondslave of Jesus Christ." The early Christians applied this designation eagerly to themselves. The word is the opposite of "free" in I Corinthians 7:21. Now the paradox: The Christian is decidedly, decisively, deliberately, definitely not free. But conversely, the Christian is definitely and decisively free! No true and free Christian ever serves Christ against his own will. You will recall that a slave happy in his master's service could voluntarily be bound to that master for life (see Exodus 21:1-6). The Christian has freely yielded himself to the possession and control of Jesus as his Savior and Master. And when Paul (and other writers in the New Testament) uses this word for himself, it does not set him apart from the rest of the believers, but identifies him as one of them. All of them happily thought of themselves as slaves of Jesus Christ.

The truth is that obedience to Christ is the fulfillment of man. This is the revelation of Jesus and the Bible, and this was Paul's Gospel — and anyone who proves it in practice finds it to be wonderfully true. Paul gloried in being a slave of Jesus Christ because it gave him a freedom undreamed of before: the freedom to fulfill his own true self.

Take a violin in your hand. That violin is a poor instrument when it is used as a sledge-hammer or a broom, because he who thus uses it obviously does not know what it is for and how to use it. Design and intention indicate purpose. In the hands of a master violinist, the violin "comes into its own," by its own "obedience" to its owner's loving and skillful employment. Man, too, is a poor instrument when owned and used by another man, or by a tyrannical system, or by himself (can you imagine a violin trying to play itself?). He "comes into his own" when He who designed him with intent and purpose and value takes him in His own hand. Man is "taken in hand" by the Master the day he is saved, and he plays out his role for the rest of his days in the manner prescribed in our text.

Our text also unwittingly confronts us with the age-old argument between those who hold two quite opposite views of salvation. One view could be called the haughty man's view of salvation (the vanity of salvation by works), and the other could be called the humble man's view of salvation (the victory of salvation by God's grace through faith in Jesus Christ). Some have tried to argue that this text supports the Pelagian view of salvation by self-effort, but a little careful examination of the text will show clearly that this is not the case.

Some people say, "I never accept anything that I haven't earned and deserved." This is sheer, utter, perfect (!) nonsense! Such a person certainly didn't earn the very gift of life itself. Furthermore, he does nothing to earn and deserve the air he breathes. And he is incapable of survival outside of the provision of God and the support of society. And he didn't cause, invent, earn or deserve any of these things! He is "a beggar at Heaven's gate" with regard to all worthwhile things, and "beggars cannot be choosers." Beggars have never been renowned for their earning power!

Note that the text does not say, "Work for your own salvation," but rather, "work out your own salvation."

Two other phrases deserve our attention before we actually explore the matter of Christian obedience. Paul reminds the Philippian believers that they had obeyed him while he was with them, and now he counsels them to obey (note that there is no object;

he does not tell them whom or what to obey) "now much more in my absence." They had rendered "eye-service" when Paul was there with them, but he encourages them to obey all the more since he has gone away from them. So Christians are to live "dependently independent lives." They are to become so dependent on the Lord that, if necessary, they can live independently of Christian leaders. And this raises the whole issue of "following the leader."

Many Christians were brought to Christ and have grown in Him under the leadership of a charismatic and dynamic Christian leader. In large measure, Paul was this type of leader. This type of leadership has both advantages and disadvantages, both delights and dangers. All Christians, both leaders and led, must be alert to the dangers and determine to live balanced lives here as in all matters of the Christian life.

Some of the dangers of charismatic, dynamic leadership in the community of believers are:

First, the temptation of clerical tyranny (absolute and unquestioned control by pastoral leaders) or clerical autocracy (this is the leader's temptation; here the pastoral leadership assumes self-rule over the Body), or the temptation of clerical worship (this is the temptation which confronts those who are led by such a leader). Both temptations are subtle and potentially deadly, and must be answered by the humble obedience (of both leader and led) featured in our text.

Second, the temptation of the leader to be the Lord's proxy or substitute. To have a pastor whom one can simply obey without argument solves a lot of problems for simple souls. Such a leader usually presents only a sterling side of his character. He never manages to confess a real sin, and thus he is always admired as if he were a perfect leader. This stance misleads both the leader and the people who are led.

Third, the temptation of unquestioning submission among the followers. This kind of submission reached its extreme in Jonestown, the cult led by Jim Jones, and the Branch Davidian compound led by David Koresh in Waco, Texas. But these are only extreme examples of those who have allowed themselves to be Satan-duped into blind following of such leaders. Most unquestioning submission to dynamic leaders is much less drastic and detectable than in those cases, but it is still very dangerous.

Paul's counsel in verse 12 of our text will provide a sure guide for us with regard to "following the leader." We will see in this study what Paul's real object was. It was to make them obedient to the Lord rather than to himself. They had been leaning on him at Philippi, perhaps (probably?) too much, when he was with them. The right business of the Christian pastor is to lead his people into a complete dependence upon the Lord. Ideally, he should do this to such a degree that he works his way out of a job. I say "ideally," because sheep will never be fully independent of their shepherds! The right way of securing this is to be the kind of man Paul was — one who himself practiced total self-commitment and obedience to Christ. He often gave such counsel as this: "Follow me — but only as I follow Christ." Nevertheless, the temptations mentioned above are always subtly present to leaders and followers.

One further item will introduce the actual study of the text. The clear and consistent Biblical view of salvation is that it operates in three grammatical tenses — the past tense, the present tense, and the future tense. Past-tense salvation ("I have been saved") is salvation in possession — once I have it, I have it forever. Present-tense salvation ("I am being saved") is salvation in process. While past-tense salvation is perfect and invariable (there are no degrees of regeneration and justification), present-tense salvation has much fluctuation and variation in it. Future-tense salvation ("I will yet be saved") is salvation in prospect — there is coming a day when I will be perfectly saved in a full, final, forever way. This will occur in the day of completed redemption that is referred to many times in the New Testament. The theological name of past-tense salvation is justification; the theological name of present-tense salvation is sanctification; and the theological name of future-tense salvation is glorification. Justification of the sinner (past-tense salvation) is gained in a crisis moment when the sinner is broken over his sins, repents of them, and trusts and receives Christ as his personal Lord and Savior. Justification is point action (it occurs at one moment of time). Sanctification, on the other hand, is gained through a continuing process. It is linear (ongoing) action, and the process must continue through every "now," every present moment of the believer's life. Glorification is also point action, beginning at a moment of time. It begins with the crisis of the believer's death, and its results continue in the Presence of God perfectly and forever.

It is important to remember as we study our text that this passage concerns only our present- tense salvation. It concerns only our sanctification. No part of this text concerns our salvation from the eternal penalty or eternal punishment of our sins (past-tense salvation). It concerns our responsibility for our own sanctification — while endowed by the Presence and power of God. Remembering that we have chosen to explore the matter of obedience from this text, we will now turn to the study itself.

THE DEMAND FOR OBEDIENCE

First, we note the *demand for obedience* that is made in the text. Verse twelve says, "Wherefore, my beloved, as ye have always obeyed, not as in my presence only, but now much more in my absence, . . ." The Greek word translated "obeyed" is based on a root word which means "to obey as a result of listening." We have already examined some matters about Christian leaders, and we will later be told in this text the importance of "the word of life." These two — Christian leaders and the Word of life — are to function together. The Christian leader's primary ministry is to "hold forth the Word of life." If God has called him to do this (pity him and his followers if He has not!), He has also called people to hear what he says. And they are to hear with a certain predisposition. They are to "hear underneath the truth" (the exact meaning of the Greek word translated "obedience"), not merely listening, and not merely appraising, but listening in full submission to Jesus as Lord as He reveals His truth. This is the word for "obedience" in the New Testament. And this is the obedience that is commanded in our text.

We see here the *responsibility* for this obedience. It is stated in these crucial words, "Work out your own salvation." This is the commanded responsibility of every Christian. There are no exemptions, exceptions, or exclusions — every Christian. Every Christian is responsible to work out his own salvation. But what does it mean to "work out your own salvation"?

The words presuppose the possession of salvation (that past-tense salvation has already occurred). The verb, "work out," is a present middle imperative verb. The present tense means that this is a present responsibility — each believer is to be doing this at every moment. The middle voice means that, as the believer fulfills his responsibility, the results (the benefits) come back to him (!). And the imperative mood means that this a command of God, a command that has equal force to any one of the Ten Commandments, or of any other command of God.

The term translated "work out" is based on the Greek word that gives us our English word "energy." This tells us that the command here insists on highly energetic action on the part of the Christian. Do we see such action generally among Christians today? No? Then we can only conclude that most dull, sluggish, inactive Christians are radically disobedient.

Now, let's explore the meaning of the words, "Work out your own salvation." I am from the state of Arkansas. Arkansas has a small town in it that bears the name, "Bauxite." That's right, Bauxite, Arkansas. You can guess its background. Years ago, it was discovered that the terrain there was rich in bauxite ore. By whatever process or crisis, God had previously worked that bauxite into the earth there. When man discovered it, he moved in and began a process of development to exploit the riches God had earlier worked into the earth. Man began to "work out" what God had already "worked in." We will look further at God's in-working later, but at the moment, we are looking at our responsibility to work out something God has already worked into us. British commentator Guy King said it beautifully: "I am to mine what is already mine." Salvation comes only by a crisis miracle of God's in-working, but once we have it, we are mutually responsible with Him to work out that which He has worked in. So present-tense salvation (sanctification) is a "co-op" between God and His child.

This can be seen Biblically in the great salvation/sanctification text of Ephesians 2:8-10. "By grace are ye saved through faith." Salvation is all of grace, but it implicates man's response of faith. "And that not of yourselves." Nothing that arises out of you can contribute to your salvation. "It is the gift of God." It has been fully provided by God Himself, free of your effort and merit. "Not of works." Your performance cannot contribute to your salvation. "Lest any man should boast." If one sinner could contribute one one-hundredth of one percent of the necessary work to gain personal salvation, heaven would never hear the last of it! He would boast all over heaven forever! But your salvation is so arranged as to totally exclude human boasting.

Paul summarizes verses eight and nine at the beginning of verse ten in the words, "For ye are God's workmanship." Then he adds the Christian's responsibility when he states, "We are God's workmanship, created in Christ Jesus unto good works, which He has previously ordained that we should walk in them."

Remember the past, present, and future tenses of our salvation. God has worked, God will work, and God is working now — and it is on the basis of His present work in us that we are to "work out our own salvation." Here is a garden. God has already worked in all the vital elements of earth and sun and rain, but a gardener must now "work it out" by breaking up the soil and planting and cultivating the flowers. There was a time when every garden was a mere opportunity or a mere possibility. The fertility of the field and the availability of the elements were gifts of God, but those gifts were improved, or "worked out," by a gardener's labor.

Here is an illustration much closer to my own heart. A noble book is a gift. It is the distilling of much wisdom gained from varying experiences of life. But before we can make it ours we must expend time, mental intensity, and persistent effort in order to "work it out." Indeed, we must "sell" all other books, for, as John Ruskin said, "If I read this book I cannot read that book." Christian, apply these illustrations to our text and you will see Paul's meaning.

There are several actions prescribed in our text which help to explain what it means to work out our salvation. The verbs are "obey" (verse 12), "shine" (verse 15), "holding forth" (verse 15), "run" (verse 16) and "labor" (verse 16). This is not intended to be an exhaustive list for "working out your own salvation" but we may take the liberty to regard it as a suggestive list. So the Christian vocation of "working out our own salvation" could involve such practical activities as obeying Christ, shining the Gospel light into a dark world, holding forth the Word of life, running the Christian race, and laboring in Christ's service. Most of these terms call for urgent, consistent, energetic action. If there is no such urgent involvement in your life, and you know that you are a Christian, you are radically disobedient. The responsibilities are to "work it out," verse 12 (this refers to your salvation); "shine it out," verse 15 (this refers to your influence), and "hold it out," verse 16 (this refers to your witness). "Work it out" is primarily a matter of character; "shine it out" involves both character and conduct, and "hold it out" (the Word of truth) involves character, conduct and communication.

To summarize: Our salvation comes solely from God; it is God's gift to us and God's accomplishment in us. However, our working it out is our acceptance of the gift and our relentless and unremitting effort to co-operate with God's grace by giving over our wills and our actions to God as He works in us. And the word that is used here, *katergazesthe* (try to pronounce that!), means to "work on to the very finish." So this is the one life's vocation that should command the attention and effort of every Christian all day long every day. This is the believer's responsibility.

Then note the *requirement* that is specified for the fulfillment of this responsibility. "Work out your own salvation in fear and trembling." At first glance, it would seem that these words enforce the secular humanist's charge of "slavery" and "slavish fear" when he evaluates the Christian duty of obedience. But first impressions are often wrong, and this is no exception. One translation renders this phrase, "with reverence and healthy respect." J. B. Philips translates it, "with a proper sense of awe and responsibility." Alan Richardson translates it, "seriously and reverently." Marvin Vincent says, "Not with slavish terror, but wholesome, serious caution." All of these are reasonable translations of the basic words.

Why does Paul put this qualifying clause with the responsibility to work out our salvation? He is fully aware of the tendency of the Christian to become casual, glib, and irreverent about the great salvation God has produced in him. The words, "How shall we escape, if we neglect so great salvation?" were not written to lost people, but to Christians! In fact, we are commanded in our text to "work out our own salvation" precisely because it is so easy to have it and neglect it. Salvation may be free, but it is not cheap! A wise Christian will not permit himself to slide into careless and disobedient living, serving and obeying his own preferences, tastes and desires more than he serves and obeys Christ. History has shown again and again that it is disastrous to be part of a Christian experience that lacks solemnity in the Presence of God and commitment in the service of Christ.

The "fear and trembling" of verse twelve are not anxiety and doubt about God, but about our own selves. When we realize how easily we can block and frustrate God's work in us by stubbornly resisting the working of His grace we must fear and tremble for the possible consequences. Our "fear and trembling" concern our awesome responsibility.

Basil, the great bishop of Cappadocia in the fourth century, wrote candidly to a friend, "I hesitate to write what I myself do in this solitude, night and day, seeing that, although I have left the distractions of the city, which are to me the occasion of innumerable evils, I have not yet succeeded in forsaking myself." The grim fight was still on for him (as for you and me), the titanic struggle to transfer his trust from self to God. Thus, the "fear and trembling" of our text — the acknowledgment of a wholesome distrust of self which will free us to trust God.

Then note the *reasons* for this obedience. Look at the word "wherefore" at the beginning of verse twelve. Actually, there are two "wherefores" in the context, one in verse nine and the one in verse twelve. The first one is found in the greatest passage on the Person of Christ in the entire Bible (verses 5-11). Humble obedience was infinitely rewarding in our Great Example, Jesus (study the "wherefore" of verse nine), and the "wherefore" of verse twelve indicates that humble obedience to Him in our lives today would have similar results. Jesus, the Son of God, was obedient while living in a world filled only with disobedient people. As a result, heaven will be full of disobedient sinners (you and I included) who became convicted and broken enough to bow at His feet, confess Him as Lord, and receive His salvation.

The introductory word "wherefore" in verse twelve dares to link our little lives with the glorious life of our exalted Lord. Paul fixes his wondering and worshiping gaze upon the humble obedience of the Lord Jesus — "He humbled Himself, and became unto death, even the death of the cross" (verse eight), and then he asks us to act in a similar way. So the first reason for our humble obedience is His humble obedience. His conduct becomes our command; His model becomes our mandate; His example becomes our exhortation.

The second reason for our obedience is found in a phrase in verse thirteen: "His good pleasure." This phrase may refer to: (l) The will of God, or (2) The pleasure, satisfaction and gratification of God. In either case, the motive of our obedience is to please and glorify Him. God Himself is pleased and gratified when we obey Him and when His purposes are accomplished (remember, His purposes are always perfect and always good). We are forever asking God to make us happy; would it not be wise if we occasionally stopped to ask Him how we can make Him happy?

One writer said, "Divine sovereignty and human responsibility meet at the crossroads of some mighty decisions. And remember, the sign marked 'His good pleasure' is the only one worth following."

The final reason for our obedience is mentioned in verse sixteen: "That I may rejoice in the day of Christ, that I have not run in vain, neither labored in vain." A Day of Evaluation is coming for every Christian, and the terms of the test are stated throughout the New Testament. The Bible reveals that each Christian will either "receive a reward" or "suffer loss," and that he will live with the result forever. Paul seems to live with his eye fixed on "that day." Even in this passage, his appeal to the Christians at Philippi is motivated by "that day." He tells them that he has made an investment (ponder that word carefully; investment is made to get a dividend, to draw interest) in them which is now at stake. Having preached to them, taught them, and discipled them, he is looking for returns "in the day of Christ" -- the day when we will receive suitable rewards for service rendered (see II Cor. 5:10). Paul's expectation of reward included not merely those to whom he has personally ministered the word of life and personally discipled in the Christian life, but also includes the number of people who will be won in turn through their soul-winning and disciple-making multiplication. So he urges them to "work out their own salvation," to "hold forth the Word of life," and to "shine as lights in a dark world." As he writes, he is gazing ahead to the "day of Christ," and he asks them to follow his gaze.

Here, then, is a lengthy look at the demand for obedience in these verses. We have looked at the Christian's responsibility of obedience, the requirement of obedience, and the reasons for obedience. Now we will go a step further.

THE DYNAMIC OF OBEDIENCE

Second, we will look at the *dynamic of obedience* that is revealed in the text. After the command to "work out your own salvation," the text then says, "For it is God which worketh in you both to will and to do of His good pleasure." So the text balances our outworking with God's in-working. God's demand to "work out your own salvation," is attended by God's dynamic, "for it is God who is working within you."

Note the *Person* Who provides this dynamic. "It is God Who works in you." You see, dear Christian, before your conversion, God worked on you by His Holy Spirit. Now, since you are saved, He works in you — by His Holy Spirit. When a sinner is saved, Jesus Christ comes into that sinner in the Presence and power of the Holy Spirit. "If any man have not the Spirit of Christ, He does not belong to him." If He is not in us, we are not Christians at all. But He is in every born-again person, and His Presence is the dynamic for this obedience and the accomplishment which comes through it. His "working in us" is the dynamic for our "working out of our salvation."

The verb of the phrase, "It is God who works in you," is a present tense, active voice verb. The present tense means that God is at work in you at this very second. Think of it! The Eternal God has stooped to work within the narrow limits of your inner life. Your heart may be as filthy as a stable, as dark as a cellar, as stifling as an over-crowded room. But He, Whom the heavens cannot contain, and in Whose sight they are not clean, is steadily at work in the unpromising, uncongenial confines of your heart. Should we not be very careful to make Him welcome, and to remove every hindrance to His work? On one occasion in the ministry of Jesus, He went into the Temple, looked around, and immediately began to overthrow all the hindrances to His free work in His House. What might He do in you, in me, today?

"God works in you." The word translated "works" is the root word from which we get our word, "energy," or "energize." It means that an energetic God lives inside of every Christian, and He is going to work every moment to fulfill His purposes there. Let this make a deep impression on your mind, Christian. The Christian life involves Divine dynamic, Divine energy, Divine work, Divine accomplishment. It is not (I repeat, not) a passive, indolent life. It was said of Jesus that "virtue went out of Him," and the same is true of Christ in you — and frankly, it will also be true of you in Him.

A close examination of the text will reveal that the word "energy" is used three times in two verses — once in verse twelve ("work out"), and twice in verse thirteen ("God is the One energizing in you to will and to energize according to His good pleasure"). The Holy Spirit made the entire passage to pulsate with energy, and that energy is the dynamic by which a Christian is to "work out his own salvation." Because there is an Energetic Worker within, there is the possibility of an energetic outworking as well. This energy is first experienced, then it is expressed. The stream flows out only because the spring rises up. Jesus implanted His life in us the day He entered our lives. And now He imparts His Presence and power to us moment by moment. He entered us then; He empowers us now. He saved us then; He sanctifies us now.

Note the *provinces* of this dynamic. Paul is even more specific about the work that Christ does in us each day. "God (emphatic) it is Who works in us, both to will and to do His good pleasure." So He works on our desires and He works on our deeds. He seeks to sanctify our desiring and our doing. And what else is there in the Christian life? So God does not do His work in us mechanically or by iron force. He works by inner promptings, inner movings, inner checkings, inner suggestions, inner inspirations, inner whispers that are delicate and sensitive. No wonder we are counseled to "Grieve not the Holy Spirit of God" (Ephesians 4:30). If we treat these inner workings with neglect or rebellion, they subside. Remember, this present-tense salvation involves a cooperation between us and the Holy Spirit.

God works in us "to will." God does not treat His children like lifeless machines. He deals with us as moral agents who can say Yes and No. He will not compel us to be saints, or force us to be holy (though He does have strong means of persuasion!). There are certain signs that God is willing His good pleasure within you -- if you have a holy discontent with yourself; if you have a hunger for a better Christian life; if you have a determination to live for "God's good pleasure." And there is a necessary conclusion that must be drawn from this truth. It means that every holy impulse that has ever been expressed within His child comes from Him, and from Him alone.

"Every virtue I possess, And every victory won,
Every thought of holiness, Are His and His alone."

But God not only inspires the will, God also energizes the work. "God works in you both to will and to do His good pleasure." He not only puts the desire into our hearts, He also provides the drive to carry out His will. He inspires the earliest impulse and He empowers and directs the final accomplishment. God leads us to purpose His will, and then He lends us the power to perform it.

Can you imagine what would happen if all Christians became aware of this truth and began to implement it in their daily lives? But we must sadly admit that this is hardly true. We are more like the truth revealed in a Dennis the Menace cartoon. Dennis is standing in his front yard with his little female "friend," Margaret. A lawn mower is standing idle in a yard that is half-cut. Dennis says indignantly to Margaret: "It is so a power mower — and here comes the power!" And he points to his father, Mr. Mitchell, who is wiping his sweating face with a towel as he comes around the corner of the house. Honesty would force many defeated Christians to say, "The Christian life may be a power-life, but I have to supply the power!" This text takes us worlds away from such a sad confession.

A father came home from work one evening to find his small son sprawled in the grass of the front yard. "Are you ready to play, son?" the father asked. The boy feebly replied, "Naw, Dad, I'm too tired." "Son, what did you do that made you so tired?" "I've been galloping on my 'horse' all over the neighborhood," the boy answering, referring to the stick-horse he sometimes played with. "Son, I've ridden a horse many times, but it has never made me that tired," the father teased. "Yeah, but Dad, your horse carries you, but when I ride, I've got to do my own galloping." Every Christian has the Lord of the universe — and all of His resources — within him, and yet most Christians are still "doing their own galloping." Who is doing the "galloping" in your life, you or God?

Let me share with you at this point a practical paragraph from the pen of the great British preacher, F. B. Meyer: "God may be working in you to confess to that fellow Christian that you were unkind in your speech or act. Work it out. He may be working in you to give up that line of business about which you have been doubtful lately. Work it out — and give it up. He may be working in you to be sweeter in your home, and gentler in your speech. Work it out — and begin. He may be working in you to alter your relations with some with whom you have dealings that are not as they should be. Work it out — and alter them. This very day let God begin to speak, and work and will; and then work out what He works in. God will not work apart from you, but He wants to work in and through you. Let Him. Yield to Him, and let this be the day when you shall begin to live in the power of the mighty Indwelling One." Amen — and may God help us!

Note one final thing about the dynamic of the Christian life. We can also see in these verses the ultimate *purpose* of this dynamic. Read verses twelve through eighteen again, and note that there is an order, a progression, to these verses. We have not mentioned much about verses fourteen through seventeen, but this in no way diminishes their importance. Here is the order:

God works in you. You co-operate with Him, "working out His in-worked salvation." Christian character is developed

This Christian character enables you to minister to others (verses 15, 16a). God's focus is on others, and the focus of the God-shaped Christian will also be on others. So we can see again the clear purpose for our Christian development. Our character is to be developed to serve others, and wonderful things develop in our character while we live to serve others. Thus, the best and happiest Christians are those who have forgotten themselves by burying their lives in the spiritual welfare of others. You see, all strength and effort that are consecrated to the service of others react upon our own character with eternal benefits.

Here, then, is the dynamic of the Christian life. We have seen the Person who provides this dynamic, the provinces in which it operates in our lives, and the ultimate purpose of it. Now, let's quickly examine one final happy thing in the text.

THE DELIGHT OF OBEDIENCE

Finally, we will look at the *delight of obedience* as it is vividly stated in our text. Let me remind you that the main theme of the book of Philippians is "joy." In fact, Greek scholar A. T. Robertson labeled this book, Paul's Joy in Christ. Guy King quaintly said that it shows us "the joy way." In verse 16, Paul used the word "rejoice." But look especially at the climax of our passage. "But even if I am being poured out as a drink offering upon the sacrifice and service of your faith, I rejoice and share my joy with you all. And you too, I urge you, rejoice in the same way and share your joy with me."

We must realize that joy is a *command* of God, and we must continually obey the command. In verse seventeen, "Rejoice," and the verb is a present imperative verb. So the Christian is commanded to rejoice — now.

We must realize, too, that to rejoice is a *choice*. Some years ago, two Christian psychologists wrote a book entitled, Happiness is a Choice. Earlier, Paul had commanded the Philippians to "do all things without murmurings and disputings" (verse 14). So Christians may choose to grumble, or they may choose not to grumble. They may choose to be argumentative, or they may choose to not be argumentative. Here, they are commanded to make the choice to rejoice. What a happy place the fellowship of believers would be if all Christians would make this choice — and say so!

We must realize, too, that rejoicing is *contagious*. The pattern of verses seventeen and eighteen never fails. "I rejoice, and share my joy with you all. And I urge you, too, to rejoice in the same way, and share your joy with me." If one person got such a good case of the contagion of joy that he couldn't hide it, many others would come down (rise up!) with it, too!

For Paul, it was joy all the way home, whatever the circumstance! The Philippian Christians are serving Christ (Paul speaks of "the sacrifice and service of their faith"), and Paul is serving Christ (he speaks of his life being freely "poured out like a drink-offering"). Note this principle: the joy is mutual when the service is mutual. The more Christians that are in the network of service, the more will be in the network of joy.

Though we didn't stop at every point along the way, our journey through this great passage is complete. We have been reminded of our salvation, of our responsibility, of our relationship to Christian leaders and their relationship to us, and of the importance of obedience in the Christian life. We have seen the demand for Christian obedience — the responsibility for it, the requirement of it, and the reasons for it. We have seen the dynamic that is necessary for us to be obedient — the Person Who gives it, the provinces in which it is exercised in our lives, and the purpose of it. And finally, we have seen the delight of Christian obedience — we have viewed that delight as a command, a choice, and a contagion. Let's close with a tiny reminder from the annals of history, an adage that stands forever: "To obey is better than sacrifice." Then let's listen to God's commands — and rise up to obey them.

Chapter 11

Timothy: a Role Model for Disciples &Disciple-Makers

But I trust in the Lord Jesus to send Timothy shortly unto you, that I also may be of good comfort, when I know your state. For I have no man like-minded, who will naturally care for your state. For all seek their own, not the things which are Jesus Christ's. But ye know the proof of him, that, as a son with the father, he hath served with me in the gospel. Him therefore I hope to send presently, so soon as I shall see how it will go with me. But I trust in the Lord that I also myself shall come shortly. (Philippians 2:19-24)

Near the end of the well-known classic story entitled <u>Good-bye, Mr. Chips</u>, as Mr. Chips lay dying, someone said, "Pity he never had any children." At that cue, Mr. Chips saw the vision of a long line of boys who had come to him in his school and gone out into life with their attitudes molded by him.* Something of this same feeling must have attended the Apostle Paul when he wrote to the Corinthians, "For though ye have ten thousand instructors in Christ, yet have ye not many fathers: for in Christ Jesus I have begotten you through the gospel" (I Corinthians 4:15). But while there was a great multitude that stood out to Paul as his spiritual children in the Lord, there was one man whom Paul considered special in a peculiar way. This man was Timothy, the son of Eunice.

There can be no question that Timothy was special as an understudy to the Apostle Paul. In six of Paul's letters Timothy's name is associated with his own in the opening lines, and in four of these Timothy's name is the only one associated with Paul's in this way.

From the beginning of their association, Timothy shared Paul's ministry on a permanent basis. Timothy was Paul's disciple, or intern, or understudy, or apprentice. Paul has been admonishing the Philippian church to practice humility in its total life. To enforce his admonition, Paul presents the examples of Jesus, of Paul himself, of Timothy, and of Epaphroditus. So Timothy is here presented as a role model to the Philippian church.

Author Randy Alcorn has written, "Much can be determined about a nation's faith and its future by the character of its role models. Who are the most admired people in America? Spiritual leaders, civic leaders, altruistic social reformers? Hardly. The heroes and idols of America are actors and actresses, jet-setters and yacht owners, star athletes, entertainers and rock stars. With a glass of wine or a joint in one hand, and somebody else's mate in the other, they prance, jiggle, curse, and swindle their way into the hearts of Americans. Our homage to such celebrities tells us as much about us — and our probable destiny — as it does them."

As I print this message, I have in hand an article from the daily newspaper of my city, dated just three days ago. The article is entitled, "Players Say Drug Use Big in the NBA." The article begins with this statement: "According to conversations with more than two dozen players, former players, agents and basketball executives, 60 to 70 percent of its 350-plus players smoke marijuana and drink excessively." "If they tested for pot, there would be no league," one player is quoted as saying. And these players are the role models for millions of American young people! Without question, Americans need to reevaluate their mental and moral standards for role models, and replace the present list with more trustworthy and exemplary individuals.

May I place Timothy before you as a possible role model? No less noteworthy a person than the Apostle Paul said, "I have no one quite like Timothy." When I consider the ministry and the magnitude of Paul, I regard this as a high commendation indeed! Let me do a brief Biblical profile of Timothy, using the total New Testament picture of him as a base.

A SON

In a peculiar way, Paul considered Timothy his own *son* in the faith. "He is to me what a son is to his father," Paul said in our text. In the brief number of Biblical references which we have to Timothy, the idea of his spiritual sonship to Paul comes out at least five times. Paul calls him "my own son in the faith," "my dearly beloved son," "son Timothy," and "Timotheus, who is my beloved son."

It is apparent from the account of Paul's first missionary journey that Paul was a leading factor in winning Timothy to faith in Jesus Christ (Acts 14:6-20). Timothy probably lived in the city of Lystra, a city which Paul visited on that first journey. The year was about A. D. 47, some 17 years after the death, burial, resurrection, and ascension of Jesus Christ. The church in Antioch had been led by the Holy Spirit to extend Christianity westward, and they selected Barnabas and Paul to be their first missionaries. They traveled westward, and everywhere they went, they not only induced faith in Jesus Christ, they also stirred up opposition to Christ and His Gospel. Lystra did not seem to be on their original itinerary; it was a replacement venue. After persecution in each of their last two stops, they walked through the city gate of the small and secluded mountain town of Lystra.

Timothy lived in a divided home in Lystra. His mother was a Jewess, and his father was a Gentile. Lystra had no synagogue, which means that the Jewish community there was very, very small. But the Holy Spirit brought Paul in contact with Timothy's God-fearing mother and grandmother, and thus with Timothy himself. Timothy may have even seen the stoning of Paul, and the Holy Spirit may have used it to stimulate a deep sympathetic interest in his heart toward Paul. No matter how it happened, it seems that Lois and Eunice, Timothy's grandmother and mother, were saved, and then young Timothy trusted Christ, also.

So Paul was Timothy's father in the faith, and Timothy was Paul's spiritual son. What does a good son do? He loves his father, respects his father, obeys his father, and shows an increasing family likeness to his father. Every growing Christian should have a spiritual son or daughter, someone he has won to Christ, and someone whom he is nurturing as a worthy parent nurtures his own children. As the parent disciples the child, the child should love his parent, grow under the administration of his parent, and carry on the work of his parent. If you are a Christian, you are someone's spiritual son or daughter. Does your spiritual father have cause to be justly proud of you as his child?

A STUDENT

We know that Timothy was a *student* just because he spent so much time with Paul. "Like father, like son," and Paul was both a great disciple of Jesus Christ and a great Christian disciple-maker. Paul wrote to the Corinthians, "Be ye imitators of me, even as I also am of Christ." Earlier in the same letter, he wrote, "I beseech you, be ye imitators of me." He writes that he is sending Timothy unto them and then says that Timothy is one "who shall put you in remembrance of my ways which are in Christ, even as I teach everywhere in every church." Timothy lived with Paul as Paul sought to imitate the example of Jesus Christ. Timothy saw the Christian life as it was set forth in the life of Paul. It became his great purpose as he saw it in Paul to live up to this ideal himself and to teach other Christians how to realize the Divine standard of character and practice in the midst of their own life situations. It was true of Timothy as it is of most men: he came to an understanding of what it means to be a Christian by observing the life of a true follower of Jesus.

After getting a "son," or a disciple — either by winning a person to Christ or adopting one who is already a Christian — the second key to disciple-making is constant, careful instruction of that disciple. In I Timothy 1:18, the Apostle Paul wrote, "Timothy, my son, I give you this instruction." The word "instruction" describes an activity Paul carried out comprehensively in Timothy's life. As an example, Paul's two recorded Epistles to Timothy are loaded with instructions on a wide variety of topics. The verse plainly declares that the instruction was aimed at helping Timothy "fight the good fight." So a Christian is not likely to be an effective Christian warrior unless he is systematically and comprehensively taught and trained in all matters of Christian truth. This teaching will be both propositional (Christian doctrine) and practical (Christian duty).

Timothy was a rare student of Scripture. Paul said to him, "Continue thou in the things which thou hast learned and hast been assured of, knowing of whom thou hast learned them; And that from a child thou hast known the holy Scriptures, which are able to make thee wise unto salvation through faith which is in Christ Jesus" (II Timothy 3:14-15). Paul also admonished Timothy to "study to show thyself approved unto God, a workman that needeth not to be ashamed, rightly dividing the word of truth," and we have every reason to believe that Timothy did exactly that. Paul encouraged Timothy to "give attendance to reading, to exhortation, to doctrine" (I Timothy 4:13), and again we may be sure he did as he was taught. According to Paul, Timothy had been "nourished up in the word of faith and of good doctrine." What a role model Timothy is for today's Christian!

Timothy was also schooled in the disciple-making process. By close observation of the Apostle Paul, by hands-on training from Paul himself, and by first-hand on-the-job training, Timothy emerged as another strong link in the disciple-making chain that stretched through the early church. Repeated exposure to the skilled disciple-making of the Apostle Paul riveted the practice in Timothy's life. Plato, the Greek philosopher, said, "Learning is remembering," and Timothy had enough great examples stored in his mind to promote lifelong learning. Dear Christian, pause just a minute and remind yourself of the many times you have seen disciple-making modeled right before your very eyes. Remember these occasions, and learn from them.

Timothy had many opportunities to see Christian unity modeled in Paul as Paul worked with Christians of every disposition and temperament, developing likeness to Christ in all of them. A first-grade Vacation Bible School teacher was a little uneasy when she saw that Davy, a boy who was visiting her class, had just one arm. She was concerned that the other children not make fun or make him feel awkward. Actually, the children did well and the class went smoothly. But toward the end of the class, the teacher herself made a thoughtless mistake. She said, "Let's close the class with our regular game — you know the one, 'Here's the church, and here's the steeple. Open the door, and here are all the people.'" The game required the use of both hands and of all the fingers. No sooner were the words out of the teacher's mouth than she remembered Davy. Before she could correct the situation, the little girl sitting next to the disabled child happily reached her hand over and said, "Here, Davy; let's build the church together!" Timothy had learned from Paul how to build the Kingdom of God and how to build individual lives in cooperative groups and in inter-networking fellowships of Christian believers. Paul's words of commendation near the end of his life indicate that Timothy had been a great student.

A SERVANT

Paul wrote of Timothy, "I have no man like-minded, who will naturally care for your state." "He is loyal, and genuinely concerned for you," another translation says. Timothy was a young man of unusual understanding, insight, and loving concern for other people. He became the very personification of the Christian ideal of servanthood. He became a kind of trouble-shooter and errand-boy for Paul, and a true *servant* of others.

Sometime ago, I read Albert Camus' tragic story entitled The Stranger, which is the picture of a man who is indifferent to (indeed, he is dead to) life and human relationships. The highest life the man can attain is a life of existence without commitment. Our modern impersonal world is increasingly filled with people like this, and the situation is unspeakably tragic. Millions progressively forfeit their destiny as true human beings by cocooning more and more within themselves. Tragically, many of these people are regular church attendants. Recently I read the sad report that three times as many Christian foreign missionaries returned home because of problems relating to other missionaries as problems relating to learning a foreign language or problems relating to cultural adjustments in the foreign country where they lived. Such relational problems are not uncommon among Christians. We must realize that no one can be a maximum Christian without developing relational skills. You will either be a bridge to God or a barrier from God to many of the people in your life.

Some of the people I admire the most are people with sensitive relational skills, people who freely relate to others. These people do not seem to be intimidated or threatened by a role of service with regard to others. In today's narcissistic and autonomous society, these people are admirable, indeed! Within the ranks of the church of Jesus Christ, relational skills and skills of service are often not admired or developed. The two greatest commandments, according to Jesus, have to do with relationships, and much of the New Testament gives guidance regarding quality relationships. The person who is sloppy, slouchy, and selfish in relationships cannot be regarded as a maturing Christian. It is the person who is relating redemptively to others who is advancing as a wise Christian. C. S. Lewis echoed Jesus when he said, "We are to keep back nothing, for nothing that we have not given away will ever be really ours."

The brother of Vincent Van Gogh, the great artist, wrote of him, "He has a great heart that is always searching for something to do for others." Van Gogh was like Paul and Timothy! The first necessity for Christian servanthood is the ability to "get alongside" all kinds of people for Christ's sake. He who walks in aloofness can never be a productive follower of Jesus Christ. The wise Christian will learn from the words of the great philosopher, Winnie the Pooh, who said,

"You can't stay in your corner of the Forest waiting for others to come to you. You have to go to them sometimes."

Harold Kushner, in his book, When All You Ever Wanted Isn't Enough, wrote, "I was sitting on a beach one summer day, watching two children, a boy and a girl, playing in the sand. They were hard at work, building an elaborate sand castle by the water's edge, with gates and towers and moats and internal passages. Just when they had nearly finished their project, a big wave came along and knocked it down, reducing it to a heap of wet sand. I expected the children to burst into tears, devastated by what had happened to all their hard work. But they surprised me. Instead, they ran up the shore away from the water, laughing and holding hands, and sat down to build another castle. I realized that they had taught me an important lesson. All the things in our lives, all the complicated structures we spend so much time and energy creating are built on sand. Only our relationships to other people endure. Sooner or later, the wave will come along and knock down what we have worked so hard to build up. When that happens, only the person who has somebody's hand to hold will be able to laugh." Every disciple and aspiring disciple-maker must learn this lesson and abide firmly by it. If you want an example of the importance of this hand-holding servanthood, get out your copy of Charles Dickens' *Tale of Two Cities* and read the concluding chapter in which Sydney Carton holds the hand of a young girl as they are being transported to the guillotine.

What was Paul's role in developing Timothy as a compassionate servant? I Timothy 1:18 contains a strange and fascinating sentence, a sentence which should be studied carefully by every disciple-maker. Paul tells Timothy that he gave his instructions to him "in keeping with the prophecies once made about Timothy." Paul had heard several people give bright predictions concerning Timothy's future as a disciple and possible Christian leader. Note that Paul did not disregard these optimistic predictions; he rather maximized them. He offered Timothy every possible opportunity to fulfill the promise he showed. On the basis of these predictions, Paul developed ambitions for Timothy. What a ministry this is — developing ambitions and assignments for other promising disciples! And what bonuses it brings to the disciple-maker as well! It builds qualitative relationships, and helps to deliver him from the sin of selfishness. Don't miss this: developing ambitions for others will help the disciple-maker to overcome the trap of self-centered individualism in ministry. By pushing others forward we develop an attitude and lifestyle which helps us to avoid pushing ourselves forward in an unhealthy way.

We must turn neutrals and enemies into friends for Christ's sake, and then we can follow Shakespeare's advice: "Those friends thou hast, and their adoption tried, grapple them to thy soul with hoops of steel."

Though this trait surely was not easy for timid Timothy, he mastered this relational skill as he saw it modeled in Paul. Timothy became a concerned and caring disciple and disciple-maker, truly a sympathetic man. He was a servant of others for Christ's sake.

A SUBSTITUTE

In developing sympathy for other people, Timothy was being prepared to play one of the most important roles of his life. As a disciple, he was a "person in training." His training prepared him for tasks that most people will miss because they have never been through hands-on disciple-training. One of Timothy's roles was something he never would have anticipated. He became a master *substitute* on God's discipleship team.

First, he was a substitute for a defecting disciple, John Mark. When Paul and Barnabas went on their first missionary journey, they took a nephew of Barnabas, John Mark, with them. However, during the journey, John Mark bailed out of the missionary enterprise and high-tailed it for home (Acts 13:13). This created such tension within Paul, and such tension between Paul and Barnabas, that they split up and formed two missionary teams for the second missionary journey. Paul selected a man named Silas, and they set out together. When they came to Lystra, Timothy's home town, they needed another helper, someone who was loyal, teachable and humble enough to do "gopher" jobs. They found exactly the kind of man they were looking for in Timothy. Timothy became John Mark's substitute on Paul's missionary team! Just think of what Mark missed when he turned his back on God's call and returned to Jerusalem! But his defection opened the door for Timothy to be substituted in his place — and to become one of God's greatest heroes. You see, John Mark began as a high-profile worker who was unproven, but Timothy began as a low-profile substitute. However, though Timothy began as a substitute, he remained a co-laborer with the great Apostle Paul for nearly twenty years. If we prove to be unfaithful to God's call to be disciples and to make disciples, Jesus said that God will take His kingdom's work away from us "and give it to those bringing forth the fruit thereof." Will you be the servant God wants, or will He put a substitute in your place?

Sometime ago, I read a great sermon by William Elliott, a Dallas Presbyterian pastor. The sermon had this fascinating title: *"Wanted: Successors to Judas."* It was based on the story in Acts one of the selection of Matthias to replace Judas among the Apostles after Judas had betrayed Christ and then had hanged himself in remorse. The premise of the sermon is that someone must rescue the many failures among the saints. Someone must "live down" those failures and their attending scandal. Someone must replace the failure with loyalty and spiritual accomplishment. So the calling of the substitute, the one who corrects failure and maintains success in the Christian life, is a very important calling. Wanted: Successors to John Mark! Successors to Judas Iscariot! Successors to Demas! Where are the Timothys today? Where are those who can pick up the broken pieces and weave them into a Christ-honoring mosaic?

But Timothy's role as substitute for John Mark only prepared him for a greater role of substitution. Incidentally, if anyone thinks to depreciate the role of a substitute, let him remember that the entire Christian Gospel in based on the idea of substitution. Jesus substituted Himself for us, taking our Hell to give us His Heaven. And now, we are to be His substitutes on earth (see II Corinthians 5:20, noting the words, "in Christ's stead"). Timothy's lowly role as

Mark's substitute prepared him for a higher role — that of being Paul's substitute.

As Timothy developed as a student and a servant, Paul gradually handed over some of his ministry to him. In Berea, Jews from Thessalonica stirred up the people so much that Paul had to leave the city. He left Timothy behind with the more veteran leader, Silas, to complete what needed to be done there (Acts 17:14-15). Later on Timothy was sent out on numerous missions as Paul's representative (or substitute). As mentioned earlier in this study, many of Paul's Epistles have Timothy's name along with his in the opening salutation. Here is the astounding picture of the senior executive, the veteran leader, acting as the public relations officer for the junior partner! No wonder the work expanded so rapidly, with such visionary and selfless leaders as Paul and such selfless sons, student, and servants as Timothy.

I read recently that "Paul almost single-handedly impacted and changed the Roman Empire." This statement has a measure of truth in it, but it is also very misleading. Paul could never have done such an amazing amount of lasting work for Christ if he had not multiplied his ministry in people like Timothy, who often served as Paul's substitute.

You see, when Paul wrote the Philippian letter, he was in prison. He wanted to come and see the Philippian brothers and sisters in person, but he was not sure of his release from prison. So he sent Timothy to them as his very own substitute. He wrote to them, "I hope to send Timothy soon to you, as soon as I find out the result of my latest hearing. But I trust in the LORD that I also myself shall come shortly." Paul wanted the Philippian Christians to know that if he could not come to them, he would send Timothy, and Timothy's coming in Paul's place would not be a reduction, because Paul had trained Timothy personally. Jesus Himself had said, "When the process of disciple-making is complete, the disciple will be like his teacher," and the Paul-Timothy relationship proved that principle. "When Timothy comes, I come. When Timothy speaks, I speak." Paul had lived transparently with Timothy, and had transferred his very life to him. This is the classic definition of New Testament disciple-making — close-up transfer of life from the disciple-maker to the disciple, and Paul and Timothy perfectly modeled this pattern. Timothy was a substitute, and he played the role with Christ-like skill.

A STEWARD

Finally, Timothy was a faithful Christian steward. The word *"steward"* describes a person who manages somebody else's goods for the advantage of the owner. Sadly, when we in today's church hear the word stewardship, we almost always think of money. But this is a severe and intolerable restriction (reduction) of the word. Stewardship includes the management of money, but that is only one small part of the full Biblical meaning of the word. In the Bible, all of life is given to each human being as a great gift from God. The recipient of the gift is to manage it for God's good and God's glory, and to fail to do so is an act of criminal embezzlement! The Bible calls it "sin." The very first sin, the "original sin," was a misappropriation of God's goods by Adam and Eve. They were given the entire garden of fruits to "tend and to keep," that is, to manage, for their own good and for God's glory. But they misappropriated to their own use the one fruit which God placed off limits, and thus they sinned. And this stewardship sin was deadly serious. That very day, they died to God.

Timothy, also, was given a stewardship charge, a responsibility to manage an estate for God's glory. He was given the greatest "trust" of all, and this trust is referred to numerous times in Paul's letters to him. The key word in picturing this trust, or stewardship, is the word, "commit." This word may also be translated, "deposit." The tracing of this stewardship in Paul's letters to Timothy is a fascinating journey.

Paul himself was a steward of the message of the Gospel of Christ, which he regarded as an incalculable treasure. The idea that may be traced in Paul's writings to Timothy is the idea of a deposit left for safekeeping in someone's care. The first stated deposit in these letters is the deposit of Paul's soul and life into Christ's care. In II Timothy 1:12, Paul wrote, "I am not ashamed, for I know whom I have believed, and am persuaded that he is able to keep that which I have committed (deposited) unto him against that day." So the first deposit in the series was the deposit of Paul's eternal welfare into Christ's hands. This is the deposit of salvation. Every Christian has made such a deposit. When he trusts Christ, he entrusts his entire eternal well-being into Christ's care. Have you been to God's Bank of Grace and deposited your entire life into Christ's safekeeping?

Then, the second deposit is made by God Himself. After Paul had deposited his soul into Christ's hands, God had entrusted (deposited) His Gospel into Paul's care. Paul wrote in I Timothy 1:11, "The glorious Gospel of the blessed God was committed (deposited) to my trust." In 1 Thessalonians 2:4, Paul wrote, "We were allowed by God to be put in trust with the Gospel." Paul was put in touch with the Gospel when God's hand of grace met his hand of faith. Then he was put in tune with it as his life began to adjust more and more to Jesus and His truth. And finally, he was put in trust with it, to be sure that it had an expansive and productive future. Never was a trustee given a greater and more responsible trust than this! "We have this treasure in earthen vessels," Paul said. The Glorious Gospel of Christ was placed into the hands of a frail man! The Eternal God suspended His earthly interests upon a mere mortal man! Paul became a carrier and communicator of the greatest of all treasures.

The third deposit in the series was made by Paul, and again the transaction was unbelievably daring and precarious. Paul deposited the Gospel that had been entrusted to him into Timothy's care! So young, timid Timothy became a link in the chain of deposits. In II Timothy 1:14, Paul counsels Timothy to "Keep (guard) by the Holy Spirit who dwells in you that good thing which was committed (deposited) unto you." Study that sentence carefully. Read it in several translations of the New Testament. Note the words, "guard," "that good thing," and "committed." The Eugene Peterson translation says, "Guard this precious thing placed in your custody by the Holy Spirit who works in us." Read this sentence again, and carefully! "Guard ... this precious thing ... placed in your custody ... by the Holy Spirit ... who works ... in us." In I Timothy 6:20, the urgency of this trust is high-lighted: "O Timothy, guard that which is deposited in your care." The last two deposits, the deposit of the Gospel to Paul, and then the deposit of the Gospel from Paul into Timothy, comprise the deposit of Gospel stewardship. You see, when a Christian owns Christ, he also immediately owes Christ. He is an instant manager, an immediate steward, of Christ and the Gospel. This is the true stewardship of Christian service.

Then, there is a final specified deposit in the ongoing chain of production and multiplication in the New Testament. Paul had deposited his soul into Christ's hands. Christ had deposited His life and His Gospel into Paul's hands. Paul had deposited the Gospel into Timothy's hands. Now, Timothy was to deposit this Gospel into the hands of faithful men, who would continue the process of Gospel advance. II Timothy 2:2 says, "And the things (the riches of the Gospel) that thou (Timothy) hast received (by deposit) from me (Paul), the same commit (deposit, entrust) to faithful men, who shall be able to teach others also." Peterson translates it, "Pass on what you heard from me to reliable leaders who are competent to teach others." Paul to Timothy to faithful men to others! Four generations of carriers and communicators, and each is as competent as the first generation because of the quality of the disciple-making process that is used to build them. This is the stewardship of succession! There is no success without succession, and there is no succession without successors! Where is your Timothy?

Look more closely for a moment at the word "commit," or "entrust," or "deposit." This is a banker's term, and it has about it an air of high-risk (and high stakes) investment. A Christian should invest (that's the word, invest) his life into some Timothy with the same care, caution, concern, and consideration that he would give to investing a large sum of money in a savings account. A great deal is at stake now and in the long-range future in such an investment.

Two great ideas are brought before us by their association with this word, "invest."

First, the word "guard," or "keep," is often used in association with this word ",deposit" in Paul's communication to Timothy. In fact, John R. W. Stott, an astute and insightful exegete of Scripture, entitled his commentary on II Timothy, <u>Guard the Gospel.</u> So the word has in it the idea of *protection*. The word suggests active diligence and intense vigilance. The Christian is the custodian of an eternal and priceless treasure, and his surveillance and custody should fit the treasure he has in his keeping. The word 'guard' (a verb, not a noun; action is required) conjures the picture of a soldier standing guard over a treasure which has been responsibly committed to him for safekeeping. Like the prison guards who guarded Paul and Silas with their own lives at stake (Acts 16); like the prison guard who carefully watched Peter (Acts 12); and like the guards who were chained to Paul to guard him in Acts 28, the Christian is "chained" to the Gospel with the lives of many at stake, and he must act suitably. Like Timothy, he is a steward.

Incidentally, there is another great idea in the background of this word, "guard," or "keep." Just like a banker guards safely the moneys, the jewels, the securities committed by his customers to his care, Almighty God keeps that which His children have deposited into His care (II Timothy 1:12)! Just as Jesus said about money in Matthew 6:19, many "thieves (would like to) break through and steal" the deposits we have made with God. But the deposit is under Triple Padlock! Colossians 3:3 says, "Ye are dead, and your life is hid with Christ in God." Furthermore, just as the United States government insures all American deposits in protected banks by means of the Federal Deposits Insurance Corporation, Heaven has its own Faith Deposits Assurance Corporation! God perfectly guarantees all deposits made with Him. I could only wish that His deposit with me would be as secure as my deposit with Him!

"Second, the word "deposit," or "invest," also has in it the idea of *propagation*. Why is a deposit of money made in a bank? To perpetuate and increase the principal! To draw a dividend! To gain interest! To multiply! This, I think, is the very reason Jesus used so many illustrations about money. Money can be multiplied by proper investment! The Gospel, a far greater treasure than any amount of money, can be multiplied by proper investment! Indeed, it must be. This is our Commission! "

I don't want to leave this word "commit" too quickly. A Bible concordance reveals that this word has a much bigger history than we would normally think. For example, it was used numerous times in the New Testament for the passing of food at a table (Mark 6:41: Mark 8:6-7; Luke 10:8; Luke 11:6; Acts 16:34; I Corinthians 10:27). The Gospel is the Bread of Life, and we are to "pass the bread" to every human being. There is a grand story in the Old Testament (II Kings 7) of four leprous men. The Syrian army was besieging their city of Samaria. They were in the "no man's land" outside the city, starving. They realized that if they went into the city, they would find no food. They knew, too, that if they remained where they were, they would still starve. They recognized, also, that if they approached the Syrian army, they would be put to death. They finally said, "Why sit we here until we die? We can only die if we act, and we will die, anyway. Let's approach the Syrians. Maybe they will pity us." So they approached the Syrian camp, only to discover that the Syrians had fled their camp in sudden fear, leaving their camp intact and unattended. The starving lepers were unexpectedly treated to a prepared banquet! With glee and gluttony, they started appropriating their newfound food and riches. Then a sudden thought disturbed them. They remembered the starving thousands shut up in the city, perishing for dire need of the supplies that were at their very fingertips. One of the lepers voiced this thought for all of them: "We do not well: this day is a day of good tidings, and we hold our peace." Friends, ours too is a Gospel day. Multitudes are starving for the Bread of Life, and we have fed — and feasted — our souls. Are we doing well or ill? Are we passing the Bread, depositing it into the hands and hearts of others?

This word, "commit," is also the word Jesus used from the Cross when He prayed, "Father, into Thy hands I commit (deposit, *entrust*) my spirit." The word is similarly used in Acts 20:32 and I Peter 4:19. Again, the word is used for the *proclamation* of Christian teaching. In Matthew 13:24, we read that "Jesus presented (committed, entrusted, deposited, invested) another parable to them..."

Finally, the word is used for the *presentation* of self and others to God. In Acts 20:32, Paul said to the Ephesian elders, "And now I commend (commit) you to God and to the word of His grace, which is able to build you up and to give you an inheritance among all those who are sanctified." In 1 Peter 4:19, Peter wrote, "Therefore, let those also who suffer according to the will of God entrust (commit, deposit) their souls to a faithful Creator in doing what is right."

Apparently, this is a gigantic stewardship with which every Christian is entrusted, and for which he is responsible. And the New Testament makes it clear that the purpose of my stewardship of the Gospel is multiplication. I am to so invest the Gospel in the lives of others through evangelism and strategic disciple-making that multiplication is guaranteed.

This principle of multiplication is revealed in many, many areas of life. Take, for example, the matter of biological cell division in a living organism. Dr. Daniel Mazia, professor of zoology at the University of California at Berkeley, said, "The rule for life is double or nothing. With few exceptions a living cell either reproduces or it dies: the principle is so simple that no one has bothered to call it a principle. A cell is born in the division of a parent cell. It then doubles in every respect: in every part, in every kind of molecule, even in the amount of water it contains." Christian, read every phrase of Dr. Mazia's statement studiously, pondering the application to Christian disciple-making. Then further consider the following biological statistics.

One fertilized human cell multiplies itself, in a mere nine months of pregnancy, no less than 120,000,000,000 times! And this does not occur haphazardly, but in such a way as to create the marvel of a human baby with all its personality and the organic complexity of its human nature built into it. You only have to think of the formation of the eye during this relatively brief period to realize what a stupendous miracle this phenomenon is. No wonder Jesus referred to His Church as His "Body." He envisioned a living organism, a "body" of living cells, each one of which is in full reproduction and leading to vast multiplication.

This, then, is the meaning of Paul's association with Timothy. This, then, is the meaning of my association with Jesus as His disciple, and my association with my own disciple. May I ask my Timothys, How are you doing in the process? Are you faithfully handling the deposit? Are you true to your entrustment? Is your sense of entitlement (what you own as a Christian) matched by a blessed sense of entrustment (what you owe as a Christian)? Timothy, how are you doing?

And, by the way, where is your Timothy? Begin to pray immediately for someone to pour your life into. When God gives you a personal Timothy, begin to spend time with him. Pray for him. Develop ambitions for him. Take him with you on your ministry assignments. Teach him what you know. Find opportunities for him to develop his ministry gifts. Be aware that there is a price to pay in handing over ministries to younger assistants. They will not, at first, do the same high-quality work as the leader. However, you must remember your own mistakes and failures as you were starting out. But mistakes and failures are "the back door to success." One day, you will stand before Jesus, and you will be glad then for all the investments you made in your Timothy.

Are you continuing as a faithful Timothy to your Paul? Aren't you grateful for him? And where is your Timothy? If you are blessed to already have a Timothy, how is he doing?

Thank you, Paul, for your investment in me.

"O Timothy, guard that which is deposited in your care."

*Here are excerpts from the closing statement of James Hilton's great classic work about teachers and their influence, <u>Goodbye, Mr. Chips:</u>

"Pity. Pity he never had any children." And at that, Chips opened his eyes as wide as he could. He struggled slowly with his words. "What — was that — you were saying — about me — just now?" "Nothing at all, old chap ... " "But — I heard you — you were talking about me --. I thought I heard one of you — saying it was a pity — a pity I never had — any children ... eh? But I have, you know ... I have ... "

And then the chorus sang in his ears in final harmony, more grandly and sweetly than he had ever heard it before, and more comfortingly too .... Pettifer, Pollett, Porson, Potts, Pullman, Purvis, Pym-Wilson, Radlett, Rapson, Reade, Reaper, Reddy Primus ... come round me now, all of you, for a last word ... Harper, Haslett, Hatfield, Hathely ... Bone, Boston, Bovey, Bradford, Bradley, Bramhall-Anderson ... wherever you are, whatever has happened, give me this moment with you ... this last moment ... my boys ..." And soon Chips was asleep.

Chapter 12

How Heaven Decorates Its War Heroes

Yet I supposed it necessary to sent to you Epaphroditus, my brother, and companion in labor, and fellow soldier, but your messenger, and he that ministered to my wants. For he longed after you all, and was full of heaviness, because that ye had heard that he had been sick. For indeed he was sick nigh unto death: but God had mercy on him; and not on him only, but on me also, lest I should have sorrow upon sorrow. I sent him therefore the more carefully, that, when ye see him again, ye may rejoice, and that I may be the less sorrowful. Receive him therefore in the Lord with all gladness; and hold such in reputation: Because for the work of Christ he was nigh unto death, not regarding his life, to supply your lack of service toward me. (Philippians 2:25-30; King James)

I have considered it desirable to send you Epaphroditus. He has been to me brother, fellow worker and comrade-in-arms, as well as being the messenger you sent to see to my wants. He has been homesick for you, and was worried because he knew that you had heard that he was ill. Indeed he was ill, very dangerously ill, but God had mercy on him — and incidentally on me as well, so that I did not have the sorrow of losing him to add to my sufferings. I am particularly anxious therefore, to send him to you so that when you see him again you may be glad, and to know of your joy will lighten my own sorrows. Welcome him in the Lord with great joy! You should hold men like him in highest honor, for his loyalty to Christ brought him very near death — he risked his life to do for me in person what distance prevented you all from doing. (Philippians 2:25-30; J. B. Phillips)

When we find the same lessons repeated again and again in the Bible, we should recognize the Holy Spirit's emphasis. The Bible does not repeat truth for the sake of filling up space, but to give it emphasis.

Philippians chapter two is the Biblical classic on the theme of humility and selfless service. In fact, this lesson is repeated at least four times in this chapter. It opens with an exhortation to such humility and service (verses 1-4). Then it continues with several personal examples of such humility and service (verses 5-30). The four examples are Christ (5-8), Paul (17), Timothy (19-24), and Epaphroditus (25-30).

There are three merely human examples in the chapter—Paul, Timothy, and Epaphroditus. When we are introduced to Epaphroditus in our text, we are brought face to face for the third time in the chapter with a mere man in whom the example of Jesus Christ shines. In fact, it seems very likely that Paul was intending to culminate and climax the exhortation to humility with the portrait of this man Epaphroditus.

If you were making a list of the greatest men and women of the Bible, there is little question that Epaphroditus would not be on the list. He was not a great leader like Moses, not a great king like David, not a distinguished prophet like Elijah, not a dynamic preacher like Peter, not a visionary missionary like Paul. Yet he was humble and selfless, and probably had the gift of "helps" (I Corinthians 12:28), a little-recognized but much-needed gift in the Body of Christ. W. H. Auden, with his usual penetrating insight, said, "The secret of most lives is in finding the right helper at the right time." Paul had the commendable relational skill of surrounding himself with good helpers, and Epaphroditus was one of them.

Paul commends this man by giving him five titles in one verse. He calls him "my brother, and companion in labor, and fellow-soldier, and your messenger, and your minister to my wants." Isolate for a moment the middle title. Epaphroditus was Paul's fellow-soldier. Paul spent a lot of time in the presence of soldiers, and he was fond of using military terminology as an analogy to the Christian life. In II Timothy 2:4, Paul exhorted Timothy to "endure hardness as a good soldier of Jesus Christ." In Ephesians 6:11-17, he encouraged all believers to put on the whole armor of God and stand against the wiles of the Devil. Paul knew of the Christian's battle against the world, the flesh, and the Devil. In this study, I want to examine the Biblical picture of Epaphroditus, who is mentioned only here and in Philippians 4:18. Then, I want to close the study by seeing "heaven's decoration of its war heroes." In looking at this man, we will consider six features—his Salvation, Service, Sympathy, Sickness, Sacrifice, and Satisfaction.

THE SALVATION WHICH HE EXHIBITED

First, we will note *the salvation he exhibited.*

We know he was saved by the place he is given in this book. However, there are two terms which should emphasize the fact that he is a Christian.

One is the *personal designation* by which he is identified throughout the paragraph. His name is "Epaphroditus," and this name is like an explanatory paragraph. It is a cultural and religious commentary all by itself. The name embodies the name of the Greek goddess Aphrodite. A mere look at his name in print or a casual pronunciation of it will reveal this. The name means "devoted to Aphrodite." It is well known that Aphrodite, or Venus as the Romans called her, was the goddess of love and beauty. Aphrodite was at the heart of a pagan religion that reveled in immorality. It is most likely that the parents of Epaphroditus were devotees of

Aphrodite, and when their little son was born they named him for their goddess.

But something radical and revolutionary happened to Epaphroditus after his birth to these Greek parents. Somewhere, perhaps at Philippi, Epaphroditus come under the preaching of the Gospel (possibly from Paul himself) and was saved. In the testimonies of men like Epaphroditus, the world has added evidence of the powerlessness of religion to save and help man, and of the power of the Gospel (Romans 1:16) to transform men's lives. Christianity is not only not a religion; it is the end of religion. Religion consists of all the things the human race has ever thought it had to do to get right with God. Christianity shows that none of them even had the least chance of doing the job, and that everything religion tried and failed to do has already been done.

Two farmers bet on their own horses in a private race. One farmer hired his own jockey and upped the ante. The other relied on lady luck. Soon after the race started, the hired jockey was far ahead. A little later, though, the other horse caught up. Near the end of the race, there was a terrible collision, and both jockeys were knocked from their horses. The seasoned jockey jumped up, remounted, and won the race. The sly farmer jumped up and down in frustration. The other farmer said, "Why are you so frustrated? You won, didn't you?" "No," replied the other farmer, "My dumb jockey got on the wrong horse!" What difference does it make that you cross the finish line way ahead — if you're riding the wrong horse? Some people are going to cross the Finish Line riding the wrong horse! Religion wins, all right — for the Devil! Man must be guarded by revealed truth, or he will slide into superstition and deception. In all religions, the emphasis is always upon man and his self-made sacrifices to appease and please God. But in the Gospel, emphasis is upon the settlement made by God's sacrifice.

As I write these words, the city of Hong Kong has taken drastic measures to purge a deadly virus from its city life. The deadly virus causes "avian flu," which is often fatal to human beings. The virus is presently being spread through poultry in Hong Kong, so the officials of the city mandated a mass slaughter of all the chickens of Hong Kong to protect the people of Hong Kong and other nations of the world. Enter religion! Last Saturday's Commercial Appeal, Memphis' daily newspaper, carried an article that included these words: "Buddhist monks and nuns began seven days of prayer and meditation for the souls of 1.3 million dead chickens last Wednesday. Shocked by the carnage, 80 monks and nuns chanted sutras, or Buddhist scriptures, and prayed to speed the birds' soul toward reincarnation." Excuse me, but I have helped many a chicken toward reincarnation, and no prayer was involved except the prayer of grace over the meal!

Epaphroditus was rescued from the treadmill of religion by a miracle of the grace and power of God through the preaching of the Gospel of Jesus Christ. Now he is truly "devoted to love," though both the devotion and the love are of a different kind. Now he will spend the rest of his life seeking to incarnate the difficult ethic of God's agape love (self-giving, self-disinterested love), and the commendation of this man in our text indicates that he is learning this ethic quite well. So his salvation is revealed in the personal designation by which he is identified.

Then his salvation is revealed in the *powerful description* which Paul attaches to him. Paul refers to him as "my brother" in our text. When Paul calls Epaphroditus by this title, he is saying something incredibly powerful. Greek scholar Kenneth Wuest says that the Greek word translated "brother" literally means, "from the same womb." It speaks of a common origin, and thus of a common level. Remember, Paul was a Jew and Epaphroditus was a Gentile. Before he became a Christian, Paul had been a proud Pharisee, and Epaphroditus would have been no more to him then than a Gentile "dog." But now, they were both born of God, so they shared the same parenthood. They were both members of God's "Forever Family," so they shared the same brotherhood. What times they must have had together in Rome! Whole nights may have been spent in telling each other of their salvation and sanctification experiences in Christ. The fact that Paul calls Epaphroditus "my brother" is an indication that the miracle of Divine salvation has occurred in each of their lives. So we see, first, the salvation Epaphroditus had exhibited.

THE SERVICE WHICH HE EXPRESSED

Next we will look at *the great service which Epaphroditus had expressed* to Paul and the Philippians. Paul referred to him (verse 25) as "my companion in labor, and fellow soldier, but your messenger, and he who ministered to my wants." Each of these terms provides a massive tribute to this man from the pen of the great Apostle Paul.

We must at least make a passing note to the personality *attributes* which enabled this man to render these great services. This man did not begrudge placing his gifts totally at the disposal of the local church in Philippi. He must have had the reputation in that local church of being completely trustworthy and willing, because the church members in Philippi were quite content to commit their money and their ministry to him. They sent their monetary gift from Philippi to Rome by way of Epaphroditus (Philippians 4:18). Incidentally, the kind of disciple you will become may well be determined by your attitude toward money, and the way you handle and manage money. Let me look into your heart and see your deepest attitude toward money, then let me read your check stubs, and I can almost tell you what kind of disciple you will be. He not only could be trusted to be a good manager of his own money; Epaphroditus was trusted to handle the offering of the entire church as well. And he did it in such a place of trust that the mishandling of it could have been excused with no accountability. He took the money on a long and arduous trip across the Roman world from Philippi to Rome, and no suspicion or question was ever raised about his personal integrity. In the Bible, the word "steward" describes one who manages the estate of another. Epaphroditus was a faithful steward. So the traits of willingness and trustworthiness are conspicuous in him.

Then we must note the *attitude* of the service he rendered. There is no question that he was a man of harmonious disposition. The words, "fellow laborer," and "fellow soldier" reveal this. I read a church sign which said, "Some people find fault as if it were buried treasure." If Epaphroditus had been a quarrelsome, nagging, fault-finding, critical person, Christian love might still allow him to be called a worker and a soldier, but he would not have been given the marvelous titles, "worker-together-with-me," and "soldier-together-with-me." This man was a gentle, cooperative, selfless servant in the cause of Christ.

Then we may note the exact *actions* he took in rendering his service. This man was no parasite, no passenger, when it came to work. It has been said that "some people are like blisters; they only show up after the work is done." But the tone of the text indicates that Epaphroditus was marked by strenuous effort and endurance. He translated his beliefs into biography! And Paul clearly states the particulars of his service. He says that Epaphroditus had been their "messenger" (verse 25). The Greek word is the word for "apostle" and it opens a whole world of understanding. The word apostle means "one sent out on a commission." The missionary traffic between Philippi and Rome was two-way traffic. One lane of the highway flowed from the church at Philippi to Paul, and the other lane flowed from Paul to the church. And all the traffic flowed through Epaphroditus.

Paul describes the traffic from the church to himself when he identifies Epaphroditus as "your messenger (apostle) and minister to my need." Epaphroditus had been their "mailman," delivering the gift of money which the Philippian church had collected and placed in his hands to take to the Apostle Paul in Rome. When Paul used the word "apostle" in describing Epaphroditus, he gave a special sacred authority to his ministry. And Epaphroditus had literally served as their mailman, delivering to Paul loving greetings and an official report of the welfare of the church in Philippi which Paul had established some years before. But Paul had used a second important word in describing the service which Epaphroditus rendered to him. He said, "He is your minister to my need." The word minister is the Greek word from which we get our word "liturgy." This word is used in the Bible to describe the Temple service of the Levitical priests. So the service of Epaphroditus had as much sacredness, in Paul's view, as the ministry of the priests in the Jewish temple services. In fact, it means that, while Epaphroditus was ministering to Paul's needs, he was actually performing an act of worship to God. And the same is true of any act of true service for Christ. Every true act of worship is an act of service, and every act of service is an act of worship.

Then Paul describes the traffic from himself to the church at Philippi when he said, "I have thought it necessary to send to you Epaphroditus ... I am the more eager to send him ... So receive him in the Lord with all joy." So Epaphroditus was truly "one sent out on a mission." At this point, he is like Jesus. The Gospel of John uses the word "sent" over forty times in describing Jesus. In fact, He referred to Himself again and again as "one sent." If a Christian is to be used of God, he must be willing to be "sent"; he must see himself as "one sent." He should never pray as to whether he should go; he should only pray as to whether he should stay. Jesus said, "As the Father hath sent Me, so send I you" (John 20:21). Paul says of Epaphroditus, "As you sent him to me, even so send I him to you." So Epaphroditus is a mailman, a missionary and a minister. What a biographical sketch! What a service he rendered to Christ, to Paul, to the Philippian believers, and to us!

THE SYMPATHY WHICH HE EXTENDED

In studying this passage about one of God's "war heroes," we must give special attention to *the sympathy he extended*. He was a sensitive and gentle giant as a man of God. In verse 26, Paul said of him, "For he longed after you all, and was full of heaviness, because that ye had heard that he had been sick." The word translated "full of heaviness" is the same word used of Jesus in the Garden of Gethsemane (Matthew 26:37). Epaphroditus was in the distress because of the concern he was causing the Christians at Philippi. This man was a living example of what Paul taught in Philippians 2:4, "Do not merely look out for your own personal interests, but also for the interests of others." He was very seriously ill, but his main concern was over how his fellow-believers in Philippi were taking the news of his illness. He was more concerned about their reaction to his serious sickness than he was about himself. As a pastor of twenty-seven years, I have sometimes seen people display this same sympathy. I have seen people involved in car accidents who were more concerned about the effect of the news on their loved ones than they were for their own welfare. I have seen a mother facing her own death by cancer who was more concerned about how her own children and loved ones were responding to the situation than she was about her own illness.

We must not forget the large figure of the Apostle Paul in the background of this paragraph. Indeed, his shadow falls big over the entire book of Philippians. Paul's presence and influence seem to create an atmosphere of sympathy and selflessness. Paul's compassion was no formal exercise of duty. It was not a detached and calculating compassion. Any student of Paul's letters can see that Paul was typically full of warm affection, true concern, and ungrudging praise. Since the Lord Jesus is the Christian's model, Paul was a model Christian.

And we must not forget that this sympathy is not automatic among Christians. Christians do not always love one another; nor are we always ready to acknowledge one another as "fellow workers" and "fellow soldiers." We sometimes look on each other with suspicion. We remain isolated and aloof from each other, fearful of guilt by association with those who have been purchased by the same precious blood. We refuse to pray with those who call on the same precious name. We sometimes begrudge the gifts God has given to others and are afraid that praise deserved by a fellow Christian might threaten our own prestige. All too often self-concern dulls our hearts to the needs of our fellow Christians. Our "eagerness" (verse 28) is directed to self-advancement, and our anxiety diminishes only as our personal security increases. How we need to see Jesus! How we need to realize His standard of humility and self-giving! How we need to follow the examples of Paul, and Timothy, and Epaphroditus! What an atmosphere of love and compassion they created. Everything outside was opposed to them; animosity and hatred were like a disease at epidemic level. But look "inside"! How Paul loved Timothy and Epaphroditus, and how Epaphroditus loved Paul and Timothy, and how they all loved the church at Philippi, and how the church at Philippi loved them! From the darkness of a Roman prison came the radiant light of a few men who lived by the power and impact of the love of God. Epaphroditus was a living extension of the sympathy and compassion he had "caught" in the exchange between Paul, his companions, and the Philippian church.

THE SICKNESS WHICH HE EXPERIENCED

Next, we will look at *the sickness which Epaphroditus had experienced.* In verse 27, Paul wrote, "He was sick nigh unto death," and again in verse 30, "He was nigh unto death." The word translated "sick" means "without strength," and is the same word that is used of Lazarus just before he died (John 11:4). The words "unto death" are the same words that are used of Jesus, "He became obedient unto death," in verse eight of this chapter. The extent of the illness is seen in these words. The exact meaning of the words is that Epaphroditus was "lying alongside of" and "near" death. "He drew near, up to death," the verse literally says. We cannot be absolutely sure of what caused the sickness, but Paul says that it was "for the work of Christ" (verse 30). And it took him "to death's door." Kenneth Wuest says that Epaphroditus and death were "next door neighbors." We need only a little imagination to see the grim struggle with death which Paul and Epaphroditus fought as this saint from Philippi lay at the point of death in a rented house in Rome.

At this point, it would be wise for us to take a minor theological excursion into the Biblical (Christian) concept of sickness. There is an incredible amount of fuzzy and erroneous teaching in the at-large Christian community which simply does not match the Bible.

First, it is necessary to remark that the presence of illness in a saint's life does not necessarily mean that there is something morally wrong between him and God which is causing the illness. The story of Lazarus (John 11) reveals that even those who Jesus especially loves sicken and die. Sickness in a believer, and the deep affection of Christ, are not incompatible. The man Jesus loves is still a man, and subject to all the frailties and mortality of manhood. The covenant of grace is not a charter of exemption. Even the saving grace of God does not lift a believer above the reach of affliction. Job 5:7 expresses the rule for all men: "Man is born unto trouble, as the sparks fly upward." It is not really strange that there is abundant sickness and suffering in such a badly fallen world; it is really strange that there is so little of it. "Strange that a harp of a thousand strings, and on a cracked instrument, should keep in tune so long." Read the ode to mortality in Ecclesiastes 12 and marvel at man's health. Because man has sinned, man suffers. The universal presence and prevalence of sickness is one of the indirect evidences that the Bible is true. All sickness is a result of sin and man's fall, but immediate sickness is not necessarily the result of some prevailing sin in the believer's life at the time of the sickness.

Second, it is vital to observe that Epaphroditus was in the presence of the Apostle Paul, and yet there is no indication that any miracle was received in his behalf. It is evident that, even in the Apostolic era, the Apostles could not perform or negotiate miracles whenever they felt so inclined.

Dr. Harry Ironside commented, "Let it be noted that the Apostle Paul did not consider he had any right to demand physical healing even for so faithful a laborer as Epaphroditus. Paul recognized the healing he received as a mercy of God, not as that to which saints have a right. This is true Divine healing. And let it be remembered that sickness may be as really from God as health. It is clear that Paul never held or taught 'healing in the atonement' and therefore the birthright of all Christians. Nor do we ever read of him or his fellow-laborers being miraculously healed."

William Hendriksen, said, "In the all-wise providence of God, believers at times become ill, sometimes gravely ill (Elisha, Hezekiah, Lazarus, Dorcas, Paul, Timothy, Trophimus, and

Epaphroditus). Yes, they get sick and they even die! The passage, 'With His stripes we are healed,' does not mean that believers have been exempted from the infirmities of the flesh, from grave illness or from death."

Then what is the purpose of God for sickness? How does His sovereignty overrule pain, and suffering, and grief, and sorrow, and death? Like a grain of sand dropped into the delicate mechanism of your eye (indeed, like sin itself), sickness and suffering are alien intruders in man's life. However, Romans 8:28 stands in the Bible for precisely such demands as sickness and death bring to life. Then what "good" is to be gleaned from such serious illness as that experienced by Epaphroditus? Let me state a massive principle: All sickness is designed to lead to healing — either spiritual healing (salvation), moral healing (repentance and correction of sin), or physical healing (whether through a miracle of restoration or the greater healing of death itself, which places us forever beyond suffering). The Psalmist wrote in Psalm 119:67, "Before I was afflicted I went astray: but now have I kept Thy word." And verse 71 adds, "It is good for me that I have been afflicted, that I might learn Thy statutes." When the final weights are put in the scales of eternity, it will be seen that The School of Adversity had the best advantages and taught the best lessons. As a frightened infant turns to its mother, or as the compass-needle turns to the Pole, so sickness should turn the believer's heart to God.

Sickness helps to remind men of death. Just as sleep is a nightly rehearsal of death, sickness is an occasional reminder of death. Sickness helps to make men think seriously of God, and the condition of their souls, and the world to come. Sickness helps to soften men's hearts, and teach them wisdom. Sickness helps to lower and humble men who are naturally proud and high-minded. Sickness helps to test men's faith, to see if it is properly placed. Sickness is God's witness, and the soul's adviser. It is an awakener of conscience and a purifier of the heart. And it should turn every Christian into a kind and sympathetic minister to others. Whatever the outcome of the sickness, the Christian should say with Paul,

"God mercied me" (the literal meaning of verse 27). When we are fallen sinners, any good thing is a bonus of God's mercy! Thank God that we have the stimulus of such stories as that of Epaphroditus in the Bible. We, too, can learn from the sickness he experienced.

THE SACRIFICE WHICH HE EXEMPLIFIED

But we have not yet reached the glorious height of this text. The height is reached when we consider *the sacrifice Epaphroditus exemplified*. Verse 30 concludes this glorious chapter with the words, *"For the work of Christ he was nigh unto death, not regarding his life, to supply your lack of service toward me."* Don't be deceived by the innocent-sounding words of the King James Bible. They actually conceal a gold mine of spiritual wealth. The key words are, *"not regarding his life."* In Greek, it is just one word. However, it has sixteen letters in it. Transliterated, it is the word, *paraboleusamenos*. You might guess that a word that long would hide a lot of meaning inside, and that is true here. This is the only place it is used in the New Testament, but outside the Bible, it had a history as a gambling term. The Revised Version translates it, *"He hazarded his life,"* but this still does not tell us the full meaning of the word. The exact and literal meaning of the word is "to wager in a game of chance." Eureka! One commentator said that it means "to gamble or bet." But remember, the gambler is Epaphroditus, and the stake is his life! To put it simply, Epaphroditus had gambled his very life to come to Rome in search of Paul. He had gambled his very life to fulfill the work he had been given to do. And he almost lost!

This same word, *parabolani*, ("The Riskers") was used a little later in church history to describe a group of Christians who ministered in the name of Christ to the sick and dying in plague-infested and disease-ridden areas, even if the diseases were contagious. A similar ministry is undertaken today by those who daringly risk their lives by hands-on ministry to AIDS victims. They minister in the full knowledge that they are risking their lives to carry on this ministry. The "Riskers" were so named because they risked disease and death to minister to stricken people in Christ's name. Paul may have had something like this in mind when he wrote to the Romans, "Greet Priscilla and Aquila, my fellow workers in Christ Jesus, who risked their own necks for my life" (Romans 16:3-4).

Epaphroditus' motive is seen in the words, "for the work of Christ." His manner is explained in the words, "he threw down his life," the very words that are used for a gambler recklessly throwing down dice in an unpredictable gamble. Paul, who was constantly with the Roman soldiers and was familiar with their reckless and regular gambling habits, came by this expression naturally. History tells us that the Roman soldier was an incurable gambler. The Apostle must have been sorely tried at times as he was forced to listen to tales of gains and losses recounted by his guards and probably had to watch their gaming often. The Roman soldier gambled on anything and everything.

One thing that makes the story of the crucifixion of Jesus so realistic is the vivid portrayal of the Roman soldiers gambling at the very foot of the cross. In fact, one artist has cleverly sketched an upturned helmet in the hands of the soldiers, ready for throwing the dice.

One of the great Christians of history was a Japanese man named Toyohiko Kagawa. Kagawa repeatedly turned down offers of wealth and position to serve Christ in the deprivation of the Shinkawa slums. An American magazine assigned a reporter to do an eight-page article on Kagawa's life. The series closed with this reporter's observation. "It appears to me," he wrote, "that Mr. Kagawa has so much security on the inside that he doesn't need any on the outside." When Kagawa was asked to explain his life, he simply replied, "Just say that I am God's Gambler." There it is! Epaphroditus was God's Gambler! He stuck his neck out, walked through an uncharted mine field, and laid his life on the line. And he did it deliberately and calculatedly, aware of the odds. In response to the worthiness of Jesus, he made himself and all he had expendable for Jesus' sake.

The greatest curse on earth today is the curse of casual, conventional, convenient Christianity, Christianity which costs nothing and produces the same. This kind of Christianity hides comfortably in its own culture and its own fortress. We simply cannot consistently talk about "the fellowship of His sufferings," or "being made conformable unto His death," unless we repent of our easy-going religious routine and join Jesus where the sound of hammer on nail may be heard. One wayfaring missionary who followed in the footsteps of Epaphroditus said, " If I really love Jesus, my innate and persistent selfishness will have received its death blow." Then he exclaimed, "Oh, for men and women who will measure their lives by what they lose and not by what they gain!"

> *"Measure your life by loss, and not by gain,*
> *Not by the wine drunk, but by the wine poured forth;*
> *For love's strength stands in love's pain,*
> *And he who suffers most may be of most worth."*

A romancing couple was seated on a dock that extended out into the Mississippi River at Vicksburg. They were dangling their feet off the dock and whispering "sweet nothings" into each other's ears when suddenly loud footfalls were heard behind them. They turned to see a man in a business suit, running at full speed toward them on the dock. They jumped up in alarm, thinking he had come to tell them of some emergency. But when he reached them, he ran right between them at full speed, and with a mighty yell, he took a flying leap toward the opposite bank of the river. Now they thought it must be a suicide attempt. But the man turned and swam powerfully back to the shore. Alarmed, the couple helped to fish him out of the water. "What in the world are you doing?" the man demanded. "What does this mean? Why did you do that?" Panting and spitting water, the drenched man pointed up to a hill above the dock. "A man up there on the hill just bet me a million to one that I couldn't jump across the Mississippi River. Now, I knew within reason that I couldn't do it — but with those odds, I couldn't just stand there and do nothing!" We seem to be in many impossible situations today. Many things God asks us to do seem impossible. But God still expects us to jump off the dock. Much of the Christian life involves "high-risk investment." The promised benefit awaits the person who is willing to run the risk. Epaphroditus provides a great example here. Christian, you may not be able to do much, but with the odds that are at stake, can you afford to just stand there and do nothing? Throw your life down, and let God sponsor the result!

If these words are being read by anyone without Christ, let me tell you the odds you face. If you bet there isn't a God, and there isn't — nothing gained, nothing lost. If you bet there isn't a God, and there is — eternal loss. If you bet there is a God, and there isn't — nothing gained, nothing lost. But if you bet there is a God, and there is — eternal gain. And remember, that everybody plays with the same stakes — everything to gain, or everything to lose. Every church should have a second name. It should call itself "The Christian Casino," the place where you go to play at high stakes, take great risks, and stand to win great benefits. And every church service should re-open the gaming table. Then every Christian could follow Epaphroditus in the sacrifice he exemplified.

THE SATISFACTION WHICH HE COULD EXPECT

Finally, we see in this story *the satisfaction Epaphroditus could expect* when he finished his time with Paul in Rome and headed back home to Philippi. After being absent for quite some time, Epaphroditus was sent back to Philippi by Paul. He was carrying with him the precious letter of Paul that we now read as the book of Philippians in our New Testament. Paul writes of the homecoming he wants Epaphroditus to receive upon his arrival in Philippi. In Philippians 2:28-29, Paul wrote, "I am sending him to you ... Receive him in the Lord with all gladness; and hold such in reputation." The New International Version says, "Welcome him in the Lord with great joy, and honor men like him." The New American Standard Version says, "Hold men like him in high regard." The term "high regard" bears major emphasis in the text, so it literally says, "Keep on holding men like him in very, very, very high regard." Do you realize what we are seeing and hearing at this point in the story? Epaphroditus is going home from the field of labor, and this lets us see what satisfaction he should be able to expect when he gets home. At this point, the story gives us a small-scale picture of the future welcome which will await men like Epaphroditus in heaven. Here is an earthly foretaste of the coming heavenly banquet. And we should give great pause here, because we should greet and welcome believers on earth the same way they will be received and welcomed in heaven. We should treat them on earth the way they will be treated in heaven. So how does heaven decorate it's war heroes?

First, heaven gives its war heroes a *royal reception*. Several times, the New Testament uses the victorious Roman general's homecoming parade as a picture of the Christian life (II Corinthians 2:14-16 & Ephesians 4:8). In every case, the war hero was given a "ticker-tape" parade, an extravagant royal welcome, a hero's reception. Acknowledgments were made about his field of battle, his military campaigns, and his victories. The same may be expected by heaven's war heroes when they reach home. Full recognition will be given to their earthly situation, and full regard will be given to their service. When Paul told the Philippians to "receive" Epaphroditus, he used a word which means to "warmly welcome." The Philippians were to welcome Epaphroditus home like a worthy war hero would expect to be welcomed upon his return home. Even so, a hero's reception awaits the faithful servant in heaven.

Second, heaven gives its war heroes a *realistic regard*. Paul told the Philippians to "hold men like him in high regard," and we may be sure that this is the policy of heaven as well as that of the church on earth. The word that is used here is also used in Luke 7:2 of the centurion's "highly-valued slave." A Christian can expect little proper regard on earth, even among other Christians. But if he is faithful and daring in his service for Christ, he is highly valued in heaven. You see, men like Epaphroditus are so unobtrusive and inconspicuous on earth that they command little attention from men.

But not so in heaven. Jesus told us again and again what gets heaven's attention and accolades. And men like Epaphroditus would be high on heaven's commendation list.

Third, heaven receives its war heroes with *real rejoicing*. If there is joy in heaven when one sinner repents, what celebration is aroused when a long-term faithful servant comes home? "Receive him with great gladness," Paul said. "Welcome him with great joy." C. S. Lewis referred to joy as "the serious business of heaven." Jonathan Edwards wrote that "every saved person is like a vessel thrown into an ocean of joy, though some vessels are far larger than others. Every vessel is full, but their capacities differ." One of God's purposes in such suffering as Epaphroditus experienced is to enlarge the believer's capacity to enjoy heaven and the glory of God. Unbelievable joy awaits heaven's war heroes.

One final thought. The word translated "receive" in verse 29 has an additional idea hidden in it. It is based on the root form *dechomai*, which includes the idea of "giving access to one's self." The Philippians were to open themselves, not just their doors, their arms, and their meetings, to Epaphroditus. We often say, "Home is where the heart is." "Home" normally includes a house in our thinking, but home is far more than a mere house. Home is an affinity of hearts. Home includes a location, but the word is reduced without loved ones at the location. Even so, when heaven's war hero arrives home, Jesus will give him access to Himself! He will not merely cross a platform or stand at a table and be recognized; he will be enfolded in the arms of the King Himself!

Let's close with a final example. Acts chapter seven records the story of the stoning of the first Christian martyr, Stephen. The name "Stephen" means "crown," and here we see him entering the coronation room! In the closing paragraph of the chapter, we find these words: "But he, being full of the Holy Spirit, looked up steadfastly into heaven, and saw the glory of God, and Jesus standing on the right hand of God, And said, Behold, I see the heavens opened, and the Son of man standing on the right hand of God. And he said, Lord Jesus, receive my spirit." Christian, read these lines with great care, asking the Holy Spirit to illumine your mind and heart as you read. "He saw the glory of God." "He saw Jesus standing at the right hand of God." "Lord Jesus, receive my spirit." Nowhere else do you see it as vividly as here. This is the only time is the New Testament where Jesus is pictured as standing at God's right hand in heaven. Elsewhere, He is always seated there, but here he is standing. It is as if he gave full recognition to Stephen's earthly situation, realistic regard to his service and his suffering, and then He acted accordingly. He stood in honor of a war hero, and personally received him into heaven with His own embrace.

Epaphroditus...

Additional thoughts on Philippians 2:25-30

The entire second chapter of Philippians is a chapter of human interest and human sympathies, of human relationships and networks of relationships. We learn here that human relationships are always dynamic, always delicate, and always demanding. They require attention, effort, self-giving, and affirmation. This chapter provides a virtual clinic on such relationships.

There are two key figures in our text. One is the Apostle Paul. Someone said, "A leader is a person with a magnet in his heart, a compass in his head, and strong cables of attachment stretched between him and other people." PAUL WAS A LEADER! The magnet in his heart adhered him to Jesus Christ, the compass in his head took him in missionary service to the ends of the earth, and the cable of attachment connected him with others who would go and serve with him.

The other key human figure in the passage is Epaphroditus, and the focus of this study is on him. The root form of the name, "Epaphroditus," means "lovely." This man was lovely in the fullest Christian sense of the word. He was full of love toward Paul and toward his friends at Philippi. His love for the apostle did not weaken his love for the Philippian brethren. Genuine love grows with every expression. You would think that love would be drained, and reduced, and depleted, with each expression, but this is not the case. A person can not diminish love by practicing it. It is not possible to reduce love by expressing it. Love is like the widow's pot of oil in II Kings 4. The more it is poured out, the more it multiplies in the vessel that it is poured from. It increases with expression.

Epaphroditus was the deputized delegate of the church in Phillippi to minister to Paul in Rome. Henry Van Dyke said, "There is a loftier ambition than merely to stand high in the world. It is to stoop down and lift mankind a little higher." Here is a triangular network of people, Paul, Epaphroditus, and the Philippians, and they all stooped to lift each other a little higher.

Think of the Christian virtues, the Christian ingredients, the Christian factors, that are exemplified here. One is joy. I read a wall motto which said,"Until further notice, celebrate everything!" The book of Philippians seems to celebrate everything. The word "joy" occurs in one of its forms some nineteen times in this book. Colorful evangelist Billy Sunday used to say, "If you have no joy, there is a leak in your Christianity somewhere." Another Christian virtue seen here is fellowship. Fellowship is the deep companionship that grows out of mutual consideration. One of the great necessities of fellowship is the necessity of keeping the links of it intact, of keeping the lines open, and of keeping the life open. In our text we can see some of the ingredients that constitute and create fellowship. In fact, this passage could be called "a formula for fellowship." Look at the ingredients.

First, common *sympathy*. Paul called Epaphroditus "my brother" and "my fellow." Fellowship is a blending of personalities, a mixing of human spirits, at the point of a mutual relationship with Jesus Christ.

Second, common *service*. It is a fallacy to think that we can have fellowship without hard work, a work that enlists every member in a common effort. Look closely at the work teams that go out from churches into mission fields — to preach, to teach, to build, to labor, etc. When they return home, they are nearer to each other than at any other time in their lives. In the early church, every member was an ex officio minister. And the work was missionary work. Examine the ministry of Jesus. His work was work-in-transit, out-going, out-moving, on-the-road work, on-the-job work. It was mobile work.

Third, common *struggle and sacrifice*. "My fellow-soldier." Each Christian is to be "more than conqueror," a "super-conqueror." He faces the universal enemies — the world, flesh, & the devil. See Phillippians 1:27-30. If we do not conquer these three enemies, they will conquer us! And we must be fellow-soldiers in facing and defeating them. Think of the courage that is exemplified in this passage. Courage does not mean the absence of fear; it means rather the presence of resources to conquer fear. It means rather that you overcome your fear in the interest of something greater than the fear. Can you imagine what it must have meant for Epaphroditus to leave his place of security and peace in Philippi and journey to Rome to stand alongside someone as unpopular as Paul was? Epaphroditus knew full well the cost of the undertaking, but he went without hesitation.

The word translated "ministered" in verse 25 comes from the Greek word from which we get the word, "liturgy." Liturgy is often used to describe worship, and especially certain forms of worship. So Paul regarded this brother's service as an offering offered gladly unto God. Epaphroditus was a "prison chaplain"; he owned one of the original "prison ministries." He was the personal chaplain to the great Apostle Paul. He knew that in ministering to the apostle he was ministering unto God. Any ministry, well-directed, is a ministry rendered unto God. Any money, well-given, is given to God.

"He was full of heaviness, because that ye had heard that he had been sick" (vs. 26). The Philippians had heard of his sickness, but they had not heard of his recovery. And his illness was dangerous and life-threatening. When the news of his illness reached the Christians in Philippi, it created a panic of anxiety among the brethren. Paul and Epaphroditus heard that they were painfully anxious, and this in turn reacted upon Epaphroditus in Rome. He agonized over being the cause of their agony. He was upset because they were upset. A Christian spirit regrets the necessity of putting sympathetic hearts to pain on his account. One of the greatest names in Christian history is the name of C.H. Spurgeon, the London preacher. Spurgeon regularly worked himself to exhaustion. When he was 58 yrs of age, he went across the English Channel to Mentone, France, which was a favorite spot to him for rest, relaxation, and recovery. It was known that he was very tired, but the world community of believers was not at all prepared for what happened. Spurgeon suddenly sickened and died while away from home. Shock waves of grief, pain, agony went out in ever-widening circles as the news of his death circulated. A massive spasm of grief ran through the Christian community in London, then England, then throughout the world. This is the kind of thing the believers in Philippi feared with regard to Epaphroditus..

Epaphroditus was a very unselfish man. He was unselfish in his sympathies, in his service, in his sacrifice, and in his sickness. His one concern in his sickness was that it should cause distress to his friends at Philippi. Some sick people have a complaining spirit that makes every one else miserable with their sufferings. Others "celebrate" their sickness in such a way as to arouse the attention and compassion of others. Some go into a "mournful mode" when they are sick, so as to arouse the maximum sympathy of others. But not Epaphroditus. He was more concerned about the reaction of the Philippians to his sufferings than he was about the sufferings themselves.

I heard about a man who had a birthday and sent his parents a telegram of congratulations! Like many people, he had a lifelong romance with himself! He was involved in an exclusive "love triangle" that involved only "me, myself, and I." Like the woman whose husband described her as "so self-centered and domineering that she now writes her diary a year in advance." In contrast, Epaphroditus was the "copy pattern" of humility and selfless service.

In verse 27, Paul said, literally, "He mercied me." He was speaking of the favor God had showed to him in sparing the life of Epaphroditus. Sometimes in mercy God spares the life of His servants; sometimes in mercy He takes them to Himself. We are in His hands, and He is the Most Merciful. He is "the Father of mercies" (II Cor 1). He knows best what is for our real good. God gave Epaphroditus more life, even as He gave to Hezekiah. "The sorrows of death compassed (surrounded) me. I was brought low, and He helped me. Return unto thy rest, O my soul, for the Lord hath dealt bountifully with thee." If we enlarge the meaning of the phrase, "He mercied me," every Christian can find his personal testimony there. I am a Christian because "He mercied me." All of my privileges and blessings are due to the fact that "He mercied me." Ray Ortlund prayed, "Oh God, when I see you most clearly, I see mercy. When I see your wrath, I see your mercy behind it. But when I see your mercy, I can discern nothing beyond, for mercy throbs at the very depths of your being. So this is where my faith finally comes to rest — in your mercy." In Isaiah 54:7, God said, "For a small moment have I forsaken thee, but with great mercies will I gather thee." Mercy is one of the spiritual bridges God has built so He can relate to you and me. Every saved person will arrive in heaven saying, "He mercied me."

"Hold such men in high honor." To honor good men is to honor God, the source of all goodness. Reverence for goodness in somebody else elevates and refines your own character. Note that Epaphroditus was only to be taken as a specimen of a class or kind of people, a category of folks. "Hold such in honor," Paul advised. We are not to honor those who have indulged themselves, but those who have given all to love and serve Christ. We know nothing of Epaphroditus beyond what this letter tells us. History tells us nothing of him, but sacred history, the Bible, tells us enough about him. You see, God even writes special books to preserve the history of men like this! Question: Where will your final record appear — merely in the perishable annals of secular history, or in the permanent records of sacred history??? Will your name only be written on the sands of time, to be erased with the passing of time, or will it be written in "God's Book of Remembrance"? (Malachi 3:16). Personally, I want to appear in God's Honor Scroll!

Note that Epaphroditus was to be fully honored when he arrived home. And he got thoroughly homesick as the time of his home-going approached. Every human being has a "homing instinct" built into his psyche. It is unspeakably tragic when this instinct is lost. I am a regular traveler. It has been my blessed privilege to make over one hundred eighty trips outside the United States, and these trips have carried me to places both near and far. I have on occasion been away from home and loved ones for weeks at a time. I can testify that I have a very live "homing instinct" in me! When a trip is being completed, the nearer I get to home, the more this instinct is activated within me. My "homing device" gives me all kinds of signals when I "turn toward home." Even so, as a Christian walks with God, his taste for home is enhanced. His homing instinct becomes more and more refined, and his homing device seems to pull him toward home with each new step.

Paul literally lavished praise and affirmation on Epaphroditus. No wonder that men were eager to risk their lives for a leader who lavished such love and praise on them. Faithful service is bought by hearty praise. A caressing hand on a horse's neck is better than a whip.

I have a beautiful but feisty Sheltie dog named "Gibbie." Gibbie and I sometimes have our differences, and he lets me know of his displeasure when a disagreement arises between us. But early each morning, he and I arise together while the rest of the household is asleep. I go to a certain seat in the den of our home, and Gibbie approaches me in ceremonial fashion. I take him in my arms and give him a brisk "rubdown of love," speaking gently to him all the while. This is one of our favorite times together, making us forget the casual and the crisis times.

Epaphroditus "threw himself" (the picture of a gambler throwing dice) into the work of supporting Paul and spreading the Gospel in Rome. He worked hard, probably in an unhealthy setting and during an unhealthy season. He willingly exposed himself to risk in order to cooperate with Paul in advancing the cause of Christ. Of the four examples of self-giving in this chapter, sacrifice is a key idea in the history of three of them, that of Christ (5-8, esp. vs. 8), that of Paul (vs. 17), and that of Epaphroditus (vs. 30). Christ was a sufferer. His sufferings have been fully documented in the Bible and in Christian history. The Bible speaks of Him as "a man of sorrows, and acquainted with grief."

Paul was a sufferer. He was a prisoner at Rome, awaiting a terrible fate, and in actual need caused by deprivation and hardship. And his affliction was totally due to his loyalty to Christ. But Paul had written, "No man should be moved by these afflictions. You yourselves know that you are appointed thereunto." General Eisenhower was right when he said, "In a war, there are no victories at bargain prices." Christians are continually at war, and there is no "safety-first" clause in the Christian contract! A ship in a harbor may be safe, but that's not what ships were built for. And Epaphroditus was a sufferer. The wording of the text means that Epaphroditus had carefully considered the possible risks and costs before he decided to go to Rome. A. T. Robertson said he risked "the Roman fever, Nero's wrath, or some unknown peril." It proved that he was risking the loss of health and the loss of life, and he seems to have considered those possible losses before he made the trip. His life and health were precious to him, but he risked them for something even more precious — the Person of Christ, and service rendered for Him and His ministers. Scottish theologian James Denney said, "The man who has nothing to die for has nothing to live for, for he does not know what life is."

Every student of Christian missions is familiar with the name of missionary C. T. Studd. Studd was one of seven great athletes of the same class in Cambridge University who went out to foreign fields to serve Christ. They were affectionately known as "the Cambridge seven." When they spoke at their home school, one undergraduate referred to them as "spiritual millionaires," and he declared that "as they spoke, the very content of the word 'sacrifice' seemed reversed. Each student present realized that the cost that he could not afford was not the cost of surrender to Christ and sacrifice for Him. The cost he could not afford was the cost of missing these things."

If you have read Leo Tolstoy's giant novel, *War and Peace*, then you know what a massive volume it is. I am always impressed when anybody tells me that they have read it, even in abridged and abbreviated form! But did you know that Tolstoy had an unacclaimed partner in the writing of it? Mrs. Tolstoy meticulously recopied all the manuscript — by hand — from his almost illegible handwriting , and she recopied some of it as many as seven times! Yet their son, Ilya, declared that she never complained! Love may labor long, and at great sacrifice — but it doesn't count the cost!

Philippi was a city where Roman conquerors once reigned, where historic battles were fought. Its very name was provided by Philip of Macedon, who was the father of Alexander the Great. So it had quite a storied history. But today, the name of the city and the names of its great people are fading dimly into history — but the name of Epaphroditus is inscribed in the Archives of Heaven and in the inspired Book of God, and history will only make it shine the brighter as people continue to open their Bibles and read Paul's letter to the Philippians.

Sometime ago, I came across the story of Dr. Claude Barlow, who, in a rare example of the love of science and of people, made himself expendable for others. Dr. Barlow had gone to Egypt, where half of the country's 19,000,000 people were suffering from a dread disease caused by tiny parasitic worms called flukes. From the irrigation ditches of the Nile, he scooped up some snails that were infested with these flukes, bottled them, and brought them to America to study them in laboratories in this country. But when he arrived back in America, the customs officials refused to allow him to bring them in. They were too dangerous, he was told. What should he do? Without lab studies, all his efforts up to this point would be in vain. Yet he couldn't carry the flukes into the country. Yes, he could! There was one way, and he took it. He swallowed the snails, and hid the parasitic flukes in his own stomach! He paid a terrible price. The pain was excruciating, just as it was for the

Egyptians. He suffered as they had suffered. The only relief he could get was from injections of a medication called "tartar emetic", which left him nauseated for eight months. Just as it did the Egyptians.

Dr. Barlow made his body the laboratory to find a way to bring healing to the Egyptians. Even so, Jesus "took our infirmities and carried our sorrows." Jesus Christ, the Son of God, took the sickness of our sins into the "laboratory" of His own body. I Peter 2:24 says, "He His Own Self carried our sins in His own body on the cross." This is the sacrifice love was willing to make. Have you received the sacrifice by faith so that it can be effective in your behalf? Have you trusted Jesus Christ personally and received Him into your life? When you trust Him, His Great Investment has begun in your life. If you have trusted Him, are you daily living so that, in a practical way, as much as humanly possible, you are "justifying" His investment?